School
Violence

OTHER BOOKS OF RELATED INTEREST

OPPOSING VIEWPOINTS SERIES
America's Youth
Gun Control
Gun Violence
Juvenile Crime
Media Violence
Teens at Risk
Violence

CURRENT CONTROVERSIES SERIES
Guns and Violence
Violence in the Media
Youth Violence

AT ISSUE SERIES
Guns and Crime
How Can Gun Violence Be Reduced?
How Can School Violence Be Prevented?
Is Media Violence a Problem?
School Shootings
Should Juveniles Be Tried as Adults?
Teen Suicide
Video Games
Violent Children

School Violence

Kate Burns, *Book Editor*

Bruce Glassman, *Vice President*
Bonnie Szumski, *Publisher*
Helen Cothran, *Managing Editor*
David M. Haugen, *Series Editor*

Contemporary Issues
Companion

GREENHAVEN PRESS
An imprint of Thomson Gale, a part of The Thomson Corporation

THOMSON
———✳———
GALE

Detroit • New York • San Francisco • San Diego • New Haven, Conn.
Waterville, Maine • London • Munich

LIBRARY OF CONGRESS CATALOGING-IN-PUBLICATION DATA

School violence / Kate Burns, book editor.
   p. cm. — (Contemporary issues companion)
  Includes bibliographical references and index.
  ISBN 0-7377-3075-7 (lib. : alk. paper) — ISBN 0-7377-3076-5 (pbk. : alk. paper)
   1. School violence—United States. I. Burns, Kate, 1969– . II. Series.
LB3013.3.S376 2005
371.7'82—dc22
                                                 2004047410

OCT 2007

CONELY BRANCH

CONTENTS

Foreword   7

Introduction   9

Chapter 1: The Nature of School Violence

1. Examining School Shooting Incidents   13
   U.S. Secret Service and U.S. Department of Education
2. Bullies in the Schoolyard   25
   Sue Smith-Heavenrich
3. School Mobbing and Emotional Abuse   31
   Gail Pursell Elliott
4. Myths About School Violence   35
   Robert C. DiGiulio

Chapter 2: The Causes of School Violence

1. Risk Factors for Violent Student Behavior   45
   Kimberly M. Williams
2. Easy Access to Guns Contributes to School Violence   54
   Centers for Disease Control and Prevention
3. Are Children with Special Needs More Likely to Commit
   School Violence?   58
   Denise (Smith) Skarbek
4. Adolescent Masculinity, Homophobia, and Violence   67
   Michael S. Kimmel and Matthew Mahler

Chapter 3: School Violence: Personal Narratives

1. Paying the Price: School Shooters Speak Out from Prison   79
   Timothy Roche and Amanda Bower
2. I Should Have Spoken Up   86
   Josh Stevens, as told to Stephanie Booth
3. School Bullies Drove My Son to Suicide   88
   Gabi Clayton
4. Confessions of a Violent Movie Writer   97
   William Mastrosimone
5. Isolation Hurts: The Perspective of a Teen-Novel Writer   102
   Chris Crutcher

Chapter 4: Preventing School Violence

1. Conflict Resolution and Peer Mediation   108
   Stephen W. Smith and Ann P. Daunic
2. The Whole School Approach to Violence Prevention   119
   Joan N. Burstyn and Rebecca Stevens

3. Preventing School Violence Aimed at Gay, Lesbian, Bisexual,
   and Transgender Youth   129
   Mark Pope
4. Helping Children Who Have Violent Tendencies   138
   Anne G. Garrett
5. Measures to Prevent the Rejection of Students by Their Peers   143
   Karen F. Osterman
6. Stopping Student Fights: An Action Plan for Teachers   148
   Lynette Fields
7. The Problem with the Expansion of Police Power in Schools   152
   Randall R. Beger

Organizations to Contact   161

Bibliography   164

Index   167

FOREWORD

In the news, on the streets, and in neighborhoods, individuals are confronted with a variety of social problems. Such problems may affect people directly: A young woman may struggle with depression, suspect a friend of having bulimia, or watch a loved one battle cancer. And even the issues that do not directly affect her private life—such as religious cults, domestic violence, or legalized gambling—still impact the larger society in which she lives. Discovering and analyzing the complexities of issues that encompass communal and societal realms as well as the world of personal experience is a valuable educational goal in the modern world.

Effectively addressing social problems requires familiarity with a constantly changing stream of data. Becoming well informed about today's controversies is an intricate process that often involves reading myriad primary and secondary sources, analyzing political debates, weighing various experts' opinions—even listening to firsthand accounts of those directly affected by the issue. For students and general observers, this can be a daunting task because of the sheer volume of information available in books, periodicals, on the evening news, and on the Internet. Researching the consequences of legalized gambling, for example, might entail sifting through congressional testimony on gambling's societal effects, examining private studies on Indian gaming, perusing numerous websites devoted to Internet betting, and reading essays written by lottery winners as well as interviews with recovering compulsive gamblers. Obtaining valuable information can be time-consuming—since it often requires researchers to pore over numerous documents and commentaries before discovering a source relevant to their particular investigation.

Greenhaven's Contemporary Issues Companion series seeks to assist this process of research by providing readers with useful and pertinent information about today's complex issues. Each volume in this anthology series focuses on a topic of current interest, presenting informative and thought-provoking selections written from a wide variety of viewpoints. The readings selected by the editors include such diverse sources as personal accounts and case studies, pertinent factual and statistical articles, and relevant commentaries and overviews. This diversity of sources and views, found in every Contemporary Issues Companion, offers readers a broad perspective in one convenient volume.

In addition, each title in the Contemporary Issues Companion series is designed especially for young adults. The selections included in every volume are chosen for their accessibility and are expertly edited in consideration of both the reading and comprehension levels of the audience. The structure of the anthologies also enhances accessibility. An introductory essay places each issue in context and provides helpful facts such as historical background or current statistics and legislation that pertain to the topic. The chapters that follow organize the material and focus on specific aspects of the book's topic. Every essay is introduced by a brief summary of its main points and biographical information about the author. These summaries aid in comprehension and can also serve to direct readers to material of immediate interest and need. Finally, a comprehensive index allows readers to efficiently scan and locate content.

The Contemporary Issues Companion series is an ideal launching point for research on a particular topic. Each anthology in the series is composed of readings taken from an extensive gamut of resources, including periodicals, newspapers, books, government documents, the publications of private and public organizations, and Internet websites. In these volumes, readers will find factual support suitable for use in reports, debates, speeches, and research papers. The anthologies also facilitate further research, featuring a book and periodical bibliography and a list of organizations to contact for additional information.

A perfect resource for both students and the general reader, Greenhaven's Contemporary Issues Companion series is sure to be a valued source of current, readable information on social problems that interest young adults. It is the editors' hope that readers will find the Contemporary Issues Companion series useful as a starting point to formulate their own opinions about and answers to the complex issues of the present day.

INTRODUCTION

On April 20, 1999, Dylan Klebold and Eric Harris detonated home-made bombs and opened fire on fellow students in the cafeteria of Columbine High School in Littleton, Colorado. They stalked the halls and library with semiautomatic weapons, assassinating twelve students and a teacher and injuring dozens more before turning their guns to end their own lives. Footage of the rampage caught on school surveillance cameras was broadcast globally, making it one of the most recognizable incidents of school violence in history. In the United States the Columbine school massacre became a watershed moment. For many the fear, dismay, and grief generated by the crime coalesced into an overwhelming jolt, and Columbine came to represent the horror inherent in all school violence. Although school violence was nothing new, the Littleton event provoked unprecedented attention on the problem and stimulated a wave of research, policy making, and activism to discover solutions.

The heightened concern since the Littleton tragedy has continued to inspire deeper scrutiny into the causes of school violence. The neighborhood surrounding Columbine High School is in the suburban community of Littleton, Colorado, a town that can be described as predominantly conservative and Caucasian. The demographics of Littleton may have little relevance when considered in isolation, but when compared to the locations of other high-profile school shootings, the similarities emerge: Many of the incidents have occurred in predominantly Caucasian suburban or rural communities. This pattern has caused some to consider whether characteristics of these communities might play a part in provoking specific forms of school violence. Some analysts have pointed to the relatively high rate of gun ownership in such neighborhoods, highlighting the fact that most school shooters obtain their guns from their own homes. Others examine the social tensions that arise in tightly knit, relatively prosperous communities where peer rejection can be devastating for teenagers. Still others ask if homogeneous communities tend to be more intolerant of anyone perceived to be different from the community norm. Like many other school shooters, Klebold and Harris were ostracized and bullied at school. Their misguided attempt to reclaim power included targeting one of the few African American students at Columbine—Isaiah Shoels—whom they addressed as "that nigger" before gunning him down. Some argue that these elements together create a culture of cruelty and exclusion that can contribute to troubled teens seeking empowerment in the barrel of a gun.

While searching for the causes of school shootings, some commentators have focused on the issue of race. Indeed, some have charged that the massive attempt to find answers itself has racial undertones. They contend that the only reason society is so concerned about the issue is that most of the perpetrators—as well as the victims—are white. Meanwhile, violence among minorities in the inner cities goes largely unnoticed. As stated by Gilda Cobb Hunter, Democratic house leader in South Carolina, "Is [school violence] an issue now because of who the victims were and who the perpetrators were? And why is it so important now that we do something when in some communities, both rural and urban, this has been an issue for a long time?"

Others have characterized the large-scale search for answers as the result of white denial. Writer Tim Wise examines how many media stories of high-profile school shootings express dismay that such violence could happen in suburban settings. In answer to news stories that ask, "What went wrong?" he speaks as a resident of white suburbia himself:

> What went wrong is that we allowed ourselves to be lulled into a false sense of security by media representations of crime and violence that portray both as the province of those who are anything but white like us. We ignore the warning signs, because in our minds the warning signs don't live in our neighborhood, but across town, in that place where we lock our car doors on the rare occasion we have to drive there. That false sense of security—the result of racist and classist stereotypes—then gets people killed. And still we act amazed.

According to Wise, the myth of white suburban purity depends on the parallel myth of minority violence.

Several important studies since the Columbine massacre have concluded that racial bias plays a key role in the public perception of violence in general. In a thorough review of news stories about criminal violence, the organization Building Blocks for Youth found: "People of color are disproportionately associated with violent crime as suspects in news stories. Six out of seven studies that examined the race of victims found a consistent underreporting of people of color as victims of crime. . . . Young people of color seem to fare as poorly as adults on the news—perhaps worse." Likewise, a study of local news broadcasts by Robert Entman found that most stories about African Americans featured them as violent criminals. Moreover, African American criminals were portrayed very differently from white criminals:

> [Black criminals] were more likely to remain unnamed, to be seen in handcuffs, in physical custody, and were less likely to speak for themselves. Thus, not only are African-Americans more likely than whites to be portrayed as criminal suspects in news stories about violent crime, but they are also more likely to be depicted as physically threatening. . . . These find-

ings strongly suggest that the media contribution is one of both linking blacks to the issue of crime and, moreover, rendering stereotypes of blacks more negative.

However, the predominant images and stories about *school* violence are about white perpetrators in white neighborhoods. Some see this development as a chance for Americans to confront the myth of minority violence. Journalist Jill Nelson argues that there is at least one useful outcome of the tragic Columbine incident: It "has brought into the open the American belief that pathological violence, like those signs at Mississippi water fountains during Jim Crow, is For Colored Only." According to Nelson, America needs a wake-up call: "The only lesson worth learning from Littleton is that violence in America pervades, crosses all boundaries and, because it is random, is inescapable. You can run, but you can't hide, and the boogeyman isn't necessarily a bro in baggy jeans. If we learned that lesson, maybe we'd be closer to doing something about it."

Like Tim Wise, Nelson asserts that the myth of suburban purity is dangerous because it prevents many white people from seriously addressing the problem of youth violence. Before Columbine, she says, too many white suburbanites believed that "if they lived in the 'burbs, in a nice house, and earned a better than decent living, they could protect their children from the violence that surrounds all Americans." The indisputable prevalence of white perpetrators in school shooting incidents may help to shatter the stereotype of minority violence and, therefore, of suburban purity.

In addition to discussions about race and school violence, *Contemporary Issues Companion: School Violence* delivers a thought-provoking assortment of research and commentary that has come into circulation since the Columbine school massacre in 1999. Sections addressing the nature, causes, and prevention of school violence contribute perspectives on the most recent debates. Personal narratives are combined with professional studies to provide a balanced collection of viewpoints and methodologies. *Contemporary Issues Companion: School Violence* offers ample material to explore meaningfully a disturbing and multifaceted problem.

CHAPTER 1

THE NATURE OF SCHOOL VIOLENCE

EXAMINING SCHOOL SHOOTING INCIDENTS

U.S. Secret Service and U.S. Department of Education

Although school shooting incidents are relatively rare, their impact on the public perception of school violence is considerable. Recognizing this fact, the U.S. Secret Service and the U.S. Department of Education joined forces to conduct an extensive study of school shooting incidents from 1974 to 2000. Published in May 2002, the *Final Report and Findings of the Safe School Initiative: Implications for the Prevention of School Attacks in the United States* compiled some of the most comprehensive information to date about the characteristics of school shooters and how they carry out their attacks. One finding is a lack of any consistent or accurate profile of school shooters. While attackers shared few identifiable physical or social traits, they did share a history of feeling bullied, persecuted, or injured by others. In most cases, their attacks were planned and prepared well in advance. Similarly, most shooters told more than one person about the attack before it occurred and displayed behavior that concerned observers. The majority of shooters had experience using guns, and many obtained the weapons used in their attacks from their own home or that of a relative.

Littleton, Colorado; Springfield, Oregon; West Paducah, Kentucky; Jonesboro, Arkansas. These communities have become familiar to many Americans as among the locations of those schools where shootings have occurred nationwide in recent years. In the aftermath of these tragic events, educators, law enforcement officials, mental health professionals and parents have pressed for answers to two central questions: "Could we have known that these attacks were being planned?" and, if so, "What could we have done to prevent these attacks from occurring?"

This publication, *The Final Report and Findings of the Safe School Ini-*

U.S. Secret Service and U.S. Department of Education, *The Final Report and Findings of the Safe School Initiative: Implications for the Prevention of School Attacks in the United States*, www.secretservice.gov, May 2002.

tiative: Implications for the Prevention of School Attacks in the United States, is a recent product of an ongoing collaboration between the U.S. Secret Service and the U.S. Department of Education to begin to answer these questions. It is the culmination of an extensive examination of 37 incidents of targeted school violence that occurred in the United States from December 1974 through May 2000. . . .

The Prevalence of Violence in American Schools

Public policymakers, school administrators, police officials and parents continue to search for explanations for the targeted violence that occurred at Columbine High School and other schools across the country, and seek assurance that similar incidents will not be repeated at educational institutions in their communities. While the quest for solutions to the problem of targeted school violence is of critical importance, reports from the Department of Education, the Justice Department and other sources indicate that few children are likely to fall prey to life-threatening violence in school settings.

To put the problem of targeted school-based attacks in context, from 1993 to 1997 the odds that a child in grades 9–12 would be threatened or injured with a weapon in school were 7 to 8 percent, or 1 in 13 or 14; the odds of getting into a physical fight at school were 15 percent, or 1 in 7. In contrast, the odds that a child would die in school by homicide or suicide are, fortunately, no greater than 1 in 1 million. In 1998, students in grades 9–12 were the victims of 1.6 million thefts and 1.2 million nonfatal violent crimes, while in this same period 60 school-associated violent deaths were reported for this student population.

The findings of the *Safe School Initiative*'s extensive search for recorded incidents of targeted school-based attacks underscore the rarity of lethal attacks in school settings. The Department of Education reports that nearly 60 million children attend the nation's 119,000+ schools. The combined efforts of the Secret Service and the Department of Education identified 37 incidents of targeted school-based attacks, committed by 41 individuals over a 25-year period.

Nevertheless, the impact of targeted school-based attacks cannot be measured in statistics alone. While it is clear that other kinds of problems in American schools are far more common than the targeted violence that has taken place in schools in this country, the high-profile shootings that have occurred in schools over the past decade have resulted in increased fear among students, parents and educators. School shootings are a rare, but significant, component of the problem of school violence. Each school-based attack has had a tremendous and lasting effect on the school in which it occurred, the surrounding community and the nation as a whole. In the wake of these attacks, fear of future targeted school violence has become a driving force behind the efforts of school officials, law enforcement professionals and parents to identify steps that can be taken to prevent incidents of violence in their schools. . . .

Characteristics of School Shooting Incidents

The *Safe School Initiative* found that targeted school violence is not a new or recent phenomenon. The earliest case that researchers were able to identify occurred in 1974. In that incident, a student brought guns and homemade bombs to his school; set off the fire alarm; and shot at emergency and custodial personnel who responded to the alarm.

The *Safe School Initiative* identified 37 incidents involving 41 attackers that met the study definition of targeted school violence and occurred between 1974 and the end of the 2000 school year. These incidents took place in 26 states, with more than one incident occurring in Arkansas, California, Kentucky, Missouri and Tennessee.

Analysis of the study findings identified the following characteristics of incidents of targeted school violence:

- In almost three-quarters of the incidents, the attacker killed one or more students, faculty or others at the school (73 percent, n=27[1]). In the remaining incidents, the attackers used a weapon to injure at least one person at school (24 percent, n=9). In one incident, a student killed his family and then held his class hostage with a weapon.
- More than one-half of the attacks occurred during the school day (59 percent, n=22), with fewer occurring before school (22 percent, n=8) or after school (16 percent, n=6).
- Almost all of the attackers were current students at the school where they carried out their attacks (95 percent, n=39). Only two attackers were former students of the school where they carried out their attacks at the time of those attacks (5 percent, n=2).
- All of the incidents of targeted school violence examined in the *Safe School Initiative* were committed by boys or young men (100 percent, n=41).
- In most of the incidents, the attackers carried out the attack alone (81 percent, n=30). In four of the incidents, the attacker engaged in the attack on his own but had assistance in planning the attack (11 percent, n=4). In three incidents, two or more attackers carried out the attack together (8 percent, n=3).
- Most attackers used some type of gun as their primary weapon, with over half of the attackers using handguns (61 percent, n=25), and nearly half of them using rifles or shotguns (49 percent, n=20). Three-quarters of the attackers used only one weapon (76

1. "N" refers to the number of attackers that corresponds to the reported percentage. Unless indicated otherwise, when the finding pertains to total attackers all n's are out of a total of 41. When the finding pertains to total incidents (i.e., school-based attacks) all n's are out of a total of 37 incidents.

percent, n=31) to harm their victims, although almost half of the attackers had more than one weapon with them at time of the attack (46 percent, n=19).

Target and Victim Characteristics

Perpetrators of incidents of targeted school violence chose a range of targets for their attacks, including fellow students, faculty and staff, and the school itself. These incidents were usually planned in advance and for most part included intent to harm a specific, pre-selected target, whether or not the attacker's execution of the incident, in fact, resulted in harm to the target.

Target and victim characteristics identified by the *Safe School Initiative* were:

- In over half of the incidents (54 percent, n=22), the attacker had selected at least one school administrator, faculty member or staff member as a target. Students were chosen as targets in fewer than half of the incidents (41 percent, n=15).
- In nearly half of the incidents, the attackers were known to have chosen more than one target prior to their attack (44 percent, n=16).
- Most attackers had a grievance against at least one of their targets prior to the attack (73 percent, n=30).
- In almost half of the incidents (46 percent, n=17), individuals who were targeted prior to the attack also became victims (i.e., individuals actually harmed in the attack). However, other individuals at the school, who were not identified as original targets of the attack, were injured or killed as well. Among these non-targeted individuals, over half were other students (57 percent, n=21) and over one-third (39 percent, n=16) were school administrators, faculty or staff. . . .

Characterizing the Attacker

Finding

There is no accurate or useful "profile" of students who engaged in targeted school violence.

Explanation

Although all of the attackers in this study were boys, there is no set of traits that described all or even most of the attackers. Instead, they varied considerably in demographic, background and other characteristics.

- The attackers ranged in age from 11 to 21, with most attackers between the ages of 13 and 18 at the time of the attack (85 percent, n=35).
- Three-quarters of the attackers were white (76 percent, n=31). One-quarter of the attackers came from other racial and ethnic backgrounds, including African American (12 percent, n=5), Hispanic (5 percent, n=2), Native Alaskan (2 percent, n=1), Native

American (2 percent, n=1), and Asian (2 percent, n=1).

The attackers came from a variety of family situations, ranging from intact families with numerous ties to the community, to foster homes with histories of neglect.

- Almost two-thirds of the attackers came from two-parent families (63 percent, n=26), living either with both biological parents (44 percent, n=18) or with one biological parent and one stepparent (19 percent, n=8).
- Some lived with one biological parent (19 percent, n=8) or split time between two biological parents (2 percent, n=1).
- Very few lived with a foster parent or legal guardian (5 percent, n=2).

For those incidents for which information on the attackers' school performance was available, that information indicates that those attackers differed considerably from one another in their academic achievement in school, with grades ranging from excellent to failing (n=34).

- The attackers in the largest grouping were doing well in school at the time of the attack, generally receiving As and Bs in their courses (41 percent; n=17); some were even taking Advanced Placement courses at the time of the incident or had been on the honor roll repeatedly.
- Fewer of the attackers were receiving Bs and Cs (15 percent, n=6), or Cs and Ds (22 percent, n=9).
- Very few of the attackers were known to be failing in school (5 percent, n=2).

Attackers also varied in the types of social relationships they had established, ranging from socially isolated to popular among their peers.

- The largest group of attackers for whom this information was available appeared to socialize with mainstream students or were considered mainstream students themselves (41 percent, n=17).
- One-quarter of the attackers (27 percent, n=11) socialized with fellow students who were disliked by most mainstream students or were considered to be part of a "fringe" group.
- Few attackers had no close friends (12 percent, n=5).
- One-third of attackers had been characterized by others as "loners," or felt themselves to be loners (34 percent, n=14).
- However, nearly half of the attackers were involved in some organized social activities in or outside of school (44 percent, n=18). These activities included sports teams, school clubs, extracurricular activities and mainstream religious groups.

Attackers' histories of disciplinary problems at school also varied. Some attackers had no observed behavioral problems, while others had multiple behaviors warranting reprimand and/or discipline.

- Nearly two-thirds of the attackers had never been in trouble or

rarely were in trouble at school (63 percent, n=26).
- One-quarter of the attackers had ever been suspended from school (27 percent, n=11).
- Only a few attackers had ever been expelled from school (10 percent, n=4).

Most attackers showed *no marked change* in academic performance (56 percent, n=23), friendship patterns (73 percent, n=30), interest in school (59 percent, n=24), or school disciplinary problems (68 percent, n=28) prior to their attack.

- A few attackers even showed some *improvements* in academic performance (5 percent, n=2) or *declines* in disciplinary problems at school (7 percent, n=3) prior to the attack. In one case, the dean of students had commended a student a few weeks before he attacked his school for improvements in his grades and a decline in the number of disciplinary problems involving that student in school.

Finding

Many attackers felt bullied, persecuted or injured by others prior to the attack.

Explanation

Almost three-quarters of the attackers felt persecuted, bullied, threatened, attacked or injured by others prior to the incident (71 percent, n=29).

In several cases, individual attackers had experienced bullying and harassment that was long-standing and severe. In some of these cases the experience of being bullied seemed to have a significant impact on the attacker and appeared to have been a factor in his decision to mount an attack at the school. In one case, most of the attacker's schoolmates described the attacker as "the kid everyone teased." In witness statements from that incident, schoolmates alleged that nearly every child in the school had at some point thrown the attacker against a locker, tripped him in the hall, held his head under water in the pool or thrown things at him. Several schoolmates had noted that the attacker seemed more annoyed by, and less tolerant of, the teasing than usual in the days preceding the attack.

Finding

A history of having been the subject of a mental health evaluation, diagnosed with a mental disorder, or involved in substance abuse did not appear to be prevalent among attackers. However, most attackers showed some history of suicidal attempts or thoughts, or a history of feeling extreme depression or desperation.

Explanation

- Only one-third of attackers had ever received a mental health evaluation (34 percent, n= 14), and fewer than one-fifth had been diagnosed with mental health or behavior disorder prior to the attack (17 percent, n=7).

- Although most attackers had not received a formal mental health evaluation or diagnosis, most attackers exhibited a history of suicide attempts or suicidal thoughts at some point prior to their attack (78 percent, n=32). More than half of the attackers had a documented history of feeling extremely depressed or desperate (61 percent, n=25).
- Approximately one-quarter of the attackers had a known history of alcohol or substance abuse (24 percent, n=10).
- The only information collected that would indicate whether attackers had been prescribed psychiatric medications concerned medication non-compliance (i.e., failure to take medication as prescribed). Ten percent of the attackers (n=4) were known to be non-compliant with prescribed psychiatric medications.

Finding

Over half of the attackers demonstrated some interest in violence, through movies, video games, books, and other media (59 percent, n=24). However, there was no one common type of interest in violence indicated. Instead, the attackers' interest in violent themes took various forms.

Explanation

- Approximately one-quarter of the attackers had exhibited an interest in violent movies (27 percent, n=11).
- Approximately one-quarter of the attackers had exhibited an interest in violent books (24 percent, n=10).
- One-eighth of the attackers exhibited an interest in violent video games (12 percent, n=5).
- The largest group of attackers exhibited an interest in violence in their own writings, such as poems, essays or journal entries (37 percent, n=15).

Finding

Most attackers had no history of prior violent or criminal behavior.

Explanation

- Fewer than one-third of the attackers were known to have acted violently toward others at some point prior to the incident (31 percent, n=13).
- Very few of the attackers were known to have harmed or killed an animal at any time prior to the incident (12 percent, n=5).
- Approximately one-quarter of the attackers had a prior history of arrest (27 percent, n=11).

Finding

Most attackers were known to have had difficulty coping with significant losses or personal failures. Moreover, many had considered or attempted suicide.

Explanation

Most attackers appeared to have difficulty coping with losses, personal failures or other difficult circumstances. Almost all of the attackers had experienced or perceived some major loss prior to the attack (98 percent, n=40). These losses included a perceived failure or loss of status (66 percent, n=27); loss of a loved one or of a significant relationship, including a romantic relationship (51 percent, n=21); and a major illness experienced by the attacker or someone significant to him (15 percent, n=6). In one case, the attacker, who was a former student at the school where the attack occurred, was laid off from his job because he did not have a high school diploma. The attacker blamed the job loss on the teacher who failed him in a senior-year course, which kept him from graduating. He returned to the school a year after leaving the school, killed his former teacher and two students, and then held over 60 students hostage for 10 hours.

For most attackers, their outward behaviors suggested difficulty in coping with loss (83 percent, n=34). For example, the mother, the brother and a friend of the attacker who lost his job each had commented that the attacker became depressed and withdrawn following the lay-off. The friend also reported that he knew that the attacker blamed his former teacher for his problems and had begun planning how to retaliate.

Conceptualizing the Attack

Finding

Incidents of targeted violence at school *rarely* are sudden, impulsive acts.

Explanation

Several findings of the *Safe School Initiative* indicate clearly that the school-based attacks studied were rarely impulsive. Rather, these attacks typically were thought out beforehand and involved some degree of advance planning. In many cases, the attacker's observable behavior prior to the attack suggested he might be planning or preparing for a school attack.

In nearly all of the incidents for which information concerning the attacker's conceptualization of the attack was available, researchers found that the attacker had developed his *idea to harm* the target(s) before the attack (95 percent, n=39). The length of time that attackers held this idea prior to the actual attack varied considerably. Some attackers conceived of the attack as few as one or two days prior to advancing that attack; other attackers had held the idea of the attack for as long as a year prior to carrying it out. For those incidents where information was available to determine how long the attacker had an idea to harm the target (n=33), the analysis showed that a little over half of the attackers developed their idea for the incident at least a month prior to the attack (51 percent, n= 17).

In addition, almost all of the attackers *planned* out the attack in advance of carrying it out (93 percent, n=38). Moreover, there was evidence from the attacker's *behavior* prior to the attack that the attacker had a plan or was preparing to harm the target(s) (93 percent, n=38). For example, one attacker asked his friends to help him get ammunition for one of his weapons; sawed off the end of a rifle to make it easier to conceal beneath his clothes; shopped for a long trench coat with his mother; and cut the pockets out of the coat so that he could conceal the weapon within the coat while holding the weapon through one of the cut-out pockets. That attacker had a well-known fascination with weapons and had told his friends on several occasions that he thought about killing certain students at school.

The length of time between the planning and execution of the attacks also varied considerably for the targeted school violence incidents studied. Some attackers developed their plans on the day of their attack or only one or two days prior; others developed their plans between six and eight months prior to the attack. In cases where there was information available to establish the date planning began (n=29), analysis of available information revealed that most of the attackers developed a plan at least two days prior to the attack (69 percent, n=21).

Revenge was a motive for more than half of the attackers (61 percent, n=25). Other motives included trying to solve a problem (34 percent, n=14); suicide or desperation (27 percent, n=11); and efforts to get attention or recognition (24 percent, n=10). More than half of the attackers had *multiple* motives or reasons for their school-based attacks (54 percent, n=22). In addition, most of the attackers held some sort of grievance at the time of the attack, either against their target(s) or against someone else (81 percent, n=33). Many attackers told other people about these grievances prior to their attacks (66 percent, n=27).

Signaling the Attack

Finding

Prior to most incidents, other people knew about the attacker's idea and/or plan to attack.

Explanation

In most cases, other people knew about the attack before it took place. In over three-quarters of the incidents, at least one person had information that the attacker was thinking about or planning the school attack (81 percent, n=30). In nearly two-thirds of the incidents, *more than one* person had information about the attack before it occurred (59 percent, n=22). In nearly all of these cases, the person who knew was a peer, a friend, schoolmate, or sibling (93 percent, n=28/30). Some peers knew exactly what the attacker planned to do; others knew something "big" or "bad" was going to happen, and in several cases knew the time and date it was to occur. An adult had information about the idea or plan in only two cases.

In one incident, for example, the attacker had planned to shoot students in the lobby of his school prior to the beginning of the school day. He told two friends exactly what he had planned and asked three others to meet him that morning in the mezzanine over-looking the lobby, ostensibly so that these students would be out of harm's way. On most mornings, usually only a few students would congregate on the mezzanine before the school day began. However, by the time the attacker arrived at school on the morning of the attack, word about what was going to happen had spread to such an extent that 24 students were on the mezzanine waiting for the attack to begin. One student who knew the attack was to occur brought a camera so that he could take pictures of the event.

Finding

Most attackers did not threaten their targets directly prior to advancing the attack.

Explanation

The majority of the attackers in the targeted school violence inci-dents examined under the *Safe School Initiative* did not threaten their target(s) directly, i.e., did not tell the target they intended to harm them, whether in direct, indirect or conditional language prior to the attack. Only one-sixth of the attackers threatened their target(s) directly prior to the attack (17 percent, n=7).

Finding

Most attackers engaged in some behavior, prior to the incident, that caused others concern or indicated a need for help.

Explanation

Almost all of the attackers engaged in some behavior prior to the attack that caused others—school officials, parents, teachers, police, fellow students—to be concerned (93 percent, n=38). In most of the cases, at least one *adult* was concerned by the attacker's behavior (88 percent, n=36). In three-quarters of the cases, at least three people—adults and other children—were concerned by the attacker's behavior (76 percent, n=31). In one case, for example, the attacker made com-ments to at least 24 friends and classmates about his interest in killing other kids, building bombs or carrying out an attack at the school. A school counselor was so concerned about this student's behavior that the counselor asked to contact the attacker's parents. The attacker's parents also knew of his interest in guns.

The behaviors that led other individuals to be concerned about the attacker included both behaviors specifically related to the attack, such as efforts to get a gun, as well as other disturbing behaviors not related to the subsequent attack. In one case, the student's English teacher became concerned about several poems and essays that the student submitted for class assignments because they treated the themes of homicide and suicide as possible solutions to his feelings of despair. In another case, the student worried his friends by talking fre-quently about plans to put rat poison in the cheese shakers at a popu-lar pizza establishment. A friend of that student became so concerned that the student was going to carry out the rat poison plan, that the friend got out of bed late one night and left his house in search of his mother, who was not home at the time, to ask her what to do.

Advancing the Attack

Finding

In many cases, other students were involved in the attack in some capacity.

Explanation

Although most attackers carried out their attacks on their own, many attackers were influenced or encouraged by others to engage in the attacks. Nearly half of the attackers were influenced by other individuals in deciding to mount an attack, dared or encouraged by others to attack, or both (44 percent; n=18). For example, one attacker's original idea had been to bring a gun to school and let other students see him with it. He wanted to look tough so that the students who had been harassing him would leave him alone. When he shared this idea with two friends, however, they convinced him that exhibiting the gun would not be sufficient and that he would have to *shoot at* people at the school in order to get the other students to leave him alone. It was after this conversation that this student decided to mount his school attack.

In other cases, friends assisted the attacker in his efforts to acquire a weapon or ammunition, discussed tactics for getting a weapon into school undetected, or helped gather information about the whereabouts of a target at a particular time during the school day.

Finding

Most attackers had access to and had used weapons prior to the attack.

Explanation

Experience using weapons and access to them was common for many attackers. Nearly two-thirds of the attackers had a known history of weapons use, including knives, guns and bombs (63 percent, n=26). Over half of the attackers had some experience specifically with a gun prior to the incident (59 percent, n=24), while others had experience with bombs or explosives (15 percent, n=6). However, fewer than half of the attackers demonstrated any fascination or excessive interest with weapons (44 percent, n=18), and less than one-third showed a fascination with explosives (32 percent, n=13) prior to their attacks. Over two-thirds of the attackers acquired the gun (or guns) used in their attacks from their own home or that of a relative (68 percent, n=28).

Resolving the Attack

Finding

Despite prompt law enforcement responses, most attacks were stopped by means other than law enforcement intervention.

Explanation

Most school-based attacks were stopped through intervention by school administrators, educators and students—or by the attacker stopping on his own. In about one-third of the incidents, the attacker was apprehended by or surrendered to administrators, faculty, or school staff (27 percent, n=10) or to students (5 percent, n=2). In just over one-fifth of the incidents, the attacker stopped on his own or left the school (22 percent, n=8). In a few incidents, the attacker killed himself during the course of the incident (13 percent, n=5).

Just over one-quarter of the incidents were stopped through law enforcement intervention (27 percent, n=10). Law enforcement personnel discharged weapons in only three of the incidents of targeted school violence studied (8 percent, n=3).

Close to half of the incidents were known to last 15 minutes or less from the beginning of the shooting to the time the attacker was apprehended, surrendered or stopped shooting (47 percent, n=16). One-quarter of the incidents were over within five minutes of their inception (27 percent, n=9). The fact that it was not through law enforcement intervention that most of the targeted school violence incidents studied were stopped appears in large part to be a function of how brief most of these incidents were in duration.

BULLIES IN THE SCHOOLYARD

Sue Smith-Heavenrich

In the following excerpt, Sue Smith-Heavenrich reports that bullying is a serious problem in schools nationwide and around the world. She describes the characteristics of bullies and the tragic consequences of bullying on both bullies and their victims. According to the author, the teasing, taunting, pushing, and shoving perpetrated by bullies not only results in emotional suffering but also frequently escalates into more serious violence. Smith-Heavenrich is a contributor to *Home Education Magazine*, a periodical that offers information and guidance on home schooling.

Bullying, often dismissed as a normal part of growing up, is a real problem in our nation's schools, according to the National School Safety Center. One out of every four schoolchildren endures taunting, teasing, pushing, and shoving daily from schoolyard bullies. More than 43 percent of middle- and high-school students avoid using school bathrooms for fear of being harassed or assaulted. Old-fashioned schoolyard hazing has escalated to instances of extortion, emotional terrorism, and kids toting guns to school.

Bullies Are Everywhere

Bullying exists in every Western or Westernized culture, from Finland and Australia to Japan and China. Three million bullying incidents are reported each year in the US alone, and over 160,000 children miss school each day for fear of being bullied. In Japan, bullying is called *ijime*. In 1993, just months before three suicides pushed *ijime* into the headlines, there were over 21,500 reported incidents of schoolyard bullying.

Many who flee urban streets to escape the culture of violence learn too late that bullying is more common in rural areas than in the cities. Researchers who surveyed hundreds of children living in the rural American Midwest found that 90 percent of middle school students and 66 percent of high school students reported having been bullied during their school careers.

Living in a culture that encourages competition and dominance, most Americans do not take bullying seriously. The problem, says

Sue Smith-Heavenrich, "Kids Hurting Kids: Bullies in the Schoolyard," *Mothering*, May/June 2001. Copyright © 2001 by Mothering Magazine. Reproduced by permission.

University of California, Los Angeles Adjunct Associate Professor of Psychology Jaana Juvonen, is that ridicule and intimidation have become acceptable. Her studies indicate that starting in middle school, bullies are considered "cool," while their victims are rejected from the social milieu.

It is estimated that more than 90 percent of all incidents of school violence begin with verbal conflicts, which escalate to profanities and then to fists or worse. Our culture has a great degree of tolerance for violence as a solution to problems. Just stroll through the local toy store; you'll find star destroyers, robots that shred their enemies, and even dolls dressed in black trench coats, wearing ski masks and toting guns. It should come as no surprise, then, that the US ranks along with England, Ireland, and Canada as having more bullies per capita than just about anywhere else in the world.

Characteristics of Bullies

A bully is someone who verbally or physically picks on others. A school bully might push you out of your seat, kick you when your back is turned, demand lunch money, threaten or insult you, call you names, or make jokes about you. A bully might give you dirty looks and spread rumors about you.

In addition to physical violence, threats, and name-calling are behaviors that qualify as emotional bullying. Excluding a child from a group or tormenting, ridiculing, and humiliating someone are kinds of emotional violence. Bullying can be racist in nature, with slurs, taunts, graffiti, and gestures. It can be sexual, with one child making abusive comments or pushing unwanted physical contact on another.

Bullies try to shame and intimidate their victims and make them feel inadequate. Some bullies are active and aggressive; others are reserved and manipulative, relying on smooth talk and lies. Bullying is not gender specific; it is estimated that 25 percent of bullies are females. Regardless of how big they are or what they look like, all bullies want power and have difficulty seeing things from another person's perspective. Simply put, bullies use other people to get what they want. Researchers are now finding out that bullies are different from other children. Their aggression begins at an early age, and they tend to attribute hostile intentions to others. They perceive provocation where none exists and set out to exact revenge. Eventually they come to believe that aggression is their best solution to conflicts.

Formerly it was accepted that bullying was rooted in low self-esteem. Recent research by UCLA's Juvonen and others reveals, however, that bullies tend to regard themselves in a positive light. Up to about sixth grade they are fairly popular, but as they get older their popularity wanes. By the time they're in high school, they tend to hang out with others like themselves: self-styled tough guys who may get what they want but are not well liked.

The person most hurt by bullying is often not the victim but the bully. The bully's behavior interferes with learning and friendships, and later on with work, relationships, income, and mental health. Children who bully tend to turn into antisocial adults and are more likely to commit crimes, batter spouses, and abuse their children. One study shows that 60 percent of boys who were bullies in middle school had at least one court conviction by the age of 24.

One researcher followed the lives of 518 individuals from the age of eight to about 50. Those children who were labeled as bullies went on to receive more driving citations and court convictions and showed higher rates of alcoholism and antisocial personality disorders. Though their intelligence level in the early grades was on a par with that of other children, by the time they were 19, their aggressive behavior interfered with developing intellectual skills. In high school, these were the children who experimented more with sex, drugs, and alcohol and had higher dropout rates.

The Hazards of Bullying

About one third of bullies are themselves victims of bullying, and a recent study shows that these children have a higher risk of depression and suicidal thoughts than other children. Clearly, being a bully can be hazardous to your health.

It is not so much the nature of the harassment, whether verbal or physical, but the extent of the bullying that harms a child. Children who are chronically targeted are likely to become increasingly withdrawn from their peers and suffer increased risk of depression and suicidal thoughts. Some actually end up killing themselves.

Nathan Feris, a seventh-grade student at Dekalb (Missouri) High School, put up with four years of teasing and taunting. He was called "chubby" and "the walking dictionary." One day in March 1987, he brought a gun to school, fatally shot another student, then took his own life. Six years later Curtis Taylor, an eighth-grade honors student from Burlington, Iowa, ended his life. He had been bullied for three years, enduring name-calling, constant tripping and shoving, and vandalism to his bicycle. In 1994, 15-year-old Brian Head walked into his classroom in Woodstock, Georgia, and shot himself. Quiet and overweight, he had been teased and bullied until he could not put up with it anymore.

Protecting Children from Bullies

The best way to protect your children is to foster their confidence and independence. You must also be willing to take action when needed. First and foremost, listen to your children. Ask them about school, social events, playtime, and sports practice. Children who are victimized by bullies may feel ashamed and too embarrassed to tell anyone, so listen to the petty gripes they bring up.

Some children don't reveal much through conversation, but other signs might alert you to the fact that all is not well. They might be afraid of walking home from school or beg for a ride instead of taking the bus. They might become withdrawn, distressed, or anxious, or come home with clothes torn and books destroyed. They may ask for extra lunch money because they are paying someone off; they may cry themselves to sleep at night.

If you think your child is being picked on, take the time to gently draw his fears out in conversation. If he mentions bullying, take his complaints seriously. First, convince him that it is not his fault, that the bully's behavior is the source of the problem. Then give him the tools to deal with the bully. Telling a child either to ignore a bully or to fight back is not the solution. Rather, we need to help our children learn to be assertive—to stand up for themselves in a nonviolent manner and have the confidence to seek help when they need it. We need to encourage action and discourage violence.

If your child is the quiet sort of victim, encourage him to express his feelings. Help him learn skills to manage his anxiety. Teach him some basic social skills: what to say and how to say it. If your child is the sort who eggs on bullies and picks unnecessary battles, teach her to "stop and think." Help her to learn more appropriate ways of expressing anger and encourage her participation in cooperative group activities.

Developing "Bully-Proof Armor"

Working together, develop some protective strategies your child can use, a sort of "bully-proof armor." In addition, teach your child to stay away from kids with bullying behavior. You may even want to enroll him or her in a martial arts school.

If your child is being bullied, it is appropriate to call the school or organization where it is happening. You should keep a record of incidents, noting dates and details. And, though you may be tempted to call the bully's parents, do not do so. Instead, try to meet the parents in a neutral environment, perhaps a classroom with a teacher or counselor present, so you can focus on solving the problem instead of blaming each other.

Patience is essential, because bullying problems are not resolved overnight. Even as we help our children develop bully-busting strategies, we must also help them strengthen talents and skills that improve their self-esteem, such as music, sports, art, math—whatever your child has a passion for and is good at. We may need to help our children develop new friendships as well as strengthen the friendships they already have. Remember, children with friends are less likely to be targets of bullies.

The last thing you want to hear is that your child is a bully. Although your normal response is to be defensive, stop for a moment, take a few deep breaths, and defuse the situation. Say something like this: "Instead of labeling my child, please tell me what happened." Then make yourself listen. Remind yourself that this discussion is ultimately about your child's wellbeing, even though it may not seem so at the moment. If your child is a bully, look for what is going on in her life to make her act this way. In talking with your child, do not blame her, and don't get pulled into a discussion about what happened or why. Instead, let her know that bullying is not acceptable in your family or in society. Offer your assistance. Ask her, "How can I help you with this? Who can you go see in school if you find yourself getting into this situation again?" Once you understand her feelings, you can teach her new ways of behaving. You can say, "If you are feeling frustrated, angry, or aggressive, here are some things you can do." Together, you can make a list and tape it to her wall. A particularly helpful activity may be to ask your child to "walk a mile" in the victim's shoes. Because bullies have trouble empathizing with their victims, it is important to discuss how it feels to be bullied.

How do you discourage a child from acting like a bully in the first place? It begins at home. Children who are treated with respect by their parents are less likely to become bullies. Never bully your children, either physically or verbally. Parents who frequently criticize their children, demand unquestioning obedience, or use spanking as punishment are sending the message that anger and intimidation are useful ways of getting what you want. Ridiculing kids, yelling at them, or ignoring them when they misbehave aren't helpful models of behavior either. Instead, use nonphysical discipline measures that are enforced consistently.

Parents who are overly permissive, who give in to obnoxious or demanding children, are letting them know that bullying pays off. Instead, teach the art of negotiation early on and help your children learn how to mediate their own disputes.

Taking Action to Stop Bullying

According to students, schools respond inadequately, if at all, to reported incidents of bullying. When Frank Barone, principal of Amsterdam High School in Amsterdam, New York, asked hundreds of eighth graders if they had ever been bullied, more than half (58.8 percent) responded in the affirmative. Yet when he asked their teachers how many students had been bullied, they put the figure at 16 percent. Clearly, adults don't recognize the extent of bullying that children face every day.

One researcher taped 52 hours of playground activity at a midsize Toronto school. She documented over 400 episodes of bullying—an average of one every seven minutes—yet teachers intervened in only one out of every 25 episodes. Another survey showed that 71 percent of teachers stayed out of or ignored incidents of teasing and bullying.

The attitudes and behaviors of teachers and school staff strongly determine the extent to which bullying manifests itself in school and on the playground. Where bullying is tolerated, it flourishes. Teachers have a tremendous amount of power to stop bullying behavior in their own classrooms by leading discussions in class. Together, students and their teacher can define bullying as unacceptable behavior, establish rules against it, and develop action plans so that students know what to do when they observe a bullying incident.

Teachers and other adults need to take immediate action when bullying does occur. They can confront bullies in private and notify the parents of both victims and bullies. Most of all, teachers can demand and model behavior grounded in respect and dignity. I've seen this work in classrooms where the teachers and students do not tolerate rude and aggressive behavior. The students feel safe, and they're excited about learning.

Schoolwide Programs

While individual teachers can teach tolerance, a better solution is to involve everyone in a schoolwide intervention program. Changing the school culture is more effective than focusing on individuals who misbehave. The best programs include both prevention and intervention. Where such programs have been implemented, the results are dramatic: bullying has decreased by up to 50 percent. Other benefits include reductions in truancy, vandalism, and fighting; improved classroom discipline; a more positive attitude toward schoolwork; and an increased satisfaction with school life among students.

McCormick Middle School, in South Carolina, adopted a program that set clear sanctions for bullies and provided counseling for both bullies and their victims. A year later, the number of students being bullied had dropped from 50 to 22 percent. Within the last three years, schools across the nation (indeed, worldwide) have been developing and implementing "bully-proofing" programs, some with snappy titles, such as "Expect Respect" or "Respect and Protect." These programs typically incorporate development of rules, discussions, role-playing, and other consciousness-raising activities into their daily routine. Some, like the one at Willow Creek Elementary School in Englewood, Colorado, depend upon the active efforts of the 80 percent of the children who are neither bullies nor victims to put a stop to the bullying.

Whatever the program, the key to success is having parents, educators, and community members work together to create a climate that clearly communicates a moral code in which cruelty is neither tolerated nor ignored.

SCHOOL MOBBING AND EMOTIONAL ABUSE

Gail Pursell Elliott

The term *mobbing* describes group-bullying behavior directed toward a common target, as Gail Pursell Elliott explains in the following excerpt from her book *School Mobbing and Emotional Abuse: See It—Stop It—Prevent It with Dignity and Respect.* Such systematic abuse from multiple perpetrators intimidates and isolates the victim, she writes, often leading to severe emotional pain and even goading the victim to take violent retribution. Many students who participate in mobbing do not realize the impact of their behavior on the victim, according to Elliott. Through education, she asserts, perpetrators and bystanders can become more aware of the dynamics of mobbing behavior and begin treating others with dignity and respect. An educator and motivational speaker, Elliott has developed mobbing awareness programs for schools.

Mobbing is group bullying. It is ganging up on someone using the tactics of rumor, innuendo, discrediting, isolating, intimidating, and above all, making it look as if the targeted person were the guilty party or instigated the behavior. As is typical of many abusive situations, the perpetrators maintain that the victim "deserved it."

The term *mobbing* may be new to you, but I'm sure you quickly recognize the behavior. If you are familiar with Stephen King's *Carrie*, Arthur Miller's *The Crucible*, or the movie *Dead Poet's Society*, you have seen examples of mobbing and what it can do.

Though the subject of books, plays, and movies, mobbing behavior is not fictional. It is real. Mobbing has a devastating effect on everyone it touches and has a ripple effect upon other people, their families, their communities, and society at large. It contributes to isolation, physical or mental illness, depression, violent or self-destructive behavior, and mistrust. The targeted person may act inappropriately due to prolonged extreme stress.

Everyone saw bullies picking on kids in the schoolyard while we were growing up. This behavior has contributed to many acts of school violence, yet no one in the United States really paid much attention to it until recently. Though mobbing and bullying in schools have been going on for many years, children were not bringing weapons to school and mass-murdering each other. It is amazing that we have been in such denial that we have to be told the obvious out loud before anyone would take action. In this case, someone had to die and a finger had to be directly pointed at this type of behavior before anyone would pay real attention to the issue.

Preventing Violence

The response to potential violence is often more reactive than proactive. Instead of creating awareness and promoting dignity and respect for all people, schools install security systems and surveillance cameras. Stiffer gun control laws are suggested. The plain truth is that many people are walking around with a deep anger inside of them and don't know why. I believe that one of the reasons is because so many have been treated like objects rather than as unique human beings for too long.

We don't have to wait until violence erupts to take action. The violence that is showcased in the media is extreme. What isn't reported is much more pervasive. Some children are afraid of riding the school bus. Some are afraid to say something because they fear retaliation. Some are excluded and humiliated. Just because a person isn't "beaten up" doesn't mean she isn't beaten up inside.

All you have to do is open the newspaper or turn on the evening news to know that we're on a collision course with something extremely unpleasant if we don't start changing the way we treat each other. Our children follow and expand upon the example we set for them.

Insight and awareness play a major role in change. So many people engage in this type of behavior without thinking. Prevention includes paying attention not only to what we're doing but also to what is going on around us. Most people don't intentionally abuse someone.

I invite you to join me in an effort to spread awareness and to help our young people. Treating others with dignity and respect, or not doing so, impacts the future for all of us.

Studying Mob Behavior

Once upon a time there was a little boy in Austria named Konrad. Like most children, Konrad loved fairy tales and folktales. There was one in particular that he found fascinating. This favorite story was about geese that joined forces when they felt threatened by a fox entering the area where they lived. They ganged up on the predator and drove it away.

When Konrad Lorenz grew up, he studied behavior in animals. Remembering the fairy tale, he decided to study this behavior in the animal kingdom and found it to be a real phenomenon. He named the behavior "mobbing" and described it as the unusual ganging up by individuals to attack another species.

School mobbing was first researched in Sweden as a result of an investigation of suicides among schoolchildren. The researchers found that the severe bullying they termed "mobbing" caused such depression and isolation among these children that some of them simply could see no other way out. In the United Kingdom, more attention currently is being paid to this behavior and the resulting suicide rate. A heart-wrenching book titled *Bullycide: Death at Playtime* tells documented, horrible tales of group abuse of children who took their own lives.

Not all who are targeted by mobbing commit suicide or acts of extreme violence. Many suffer in silence. They are confused, isolated, and depressed, and they grow up lacking the self-confidence to realize their full potential. Those who suffer and still excel in work or higher education carry with them the memory of their experience. There is always injury, and the experience leaves permanent scars.

When I give presentations to groups of adults on this subject, I ask how many had this happen to them when they were in school. At least half of the audience invariably raises their hands. When I ask how many of them can remember the names of the students who encouraged or perpetrated the abuse, everyone remembers. When I ask why they believe that this happened to them, not one of them really knows why. Some still wonder what they did that caused others to gang up on them and hurt them like that.

Mobbing is always caused by some sort of basic conflict, usually something impersonal that became extremely personal in terms of outcome. It can be anything. Someone says the wrong thing at the wrong time. Someone is new to the school. Someone looks, acts, or talks differently. Someone is very smart or the opposite. Someone brags about his or her family. Someone wears clothes that are different or not the current style.

Regardless of what the cause is, the mobbers use it as an excuse to engage in emotional abuse and to treat the target as a "sort of a person" rather than as a human being with wants, hopes, needs, dreams, and desires. Long after the initial conflict is forgotten, the mobbing continues. I think that if you asked those who participated why they did, they would be unable to give you a credible explanation.

The truth is that it doesn't matter what nameless phantom of misunderstanding triggers mobbing. No one deserves to be abused and treated like an object. No one. And it must stop, or everyone is at risk. Everyone. . . .

Chicken Pecking

Mobbing has often been likened to chicken pecking, a form of barnyard behavior. Chicken pecking is not one large chicken bullying a smaller chicken and beating on it. All the chickens target and isolate one chick and randomly go over and peck it once, maybe twice. Not one of them abuses the chick enough to really do harm. But eventually the chicken dies because of the accumulation of all the pecks.

- When chicken pecking occurs, the target never comes back and retaliates.
- When the chicken dies, the other chickens don't look at each other in shock or surprise. They know exactly what they are doing.

When a student is being mobbed by other students, minor incidents of ridicule or shunning may occur. It is the accumulation of so many students engaging in the same behavior that causes the spirit and self-image of the target to be in danger of perishing.

When the research on workplace mobbing was done in Sweden in the 1980s and the researchers went back into the workplace and explained to coworkers what the consequences to the individual were as a result of their actions, the coworkers were shocked and appalled that they could have participated in anything that would have damaged another person to that extent. "But all I did was . . ." Just one or two pecks. But there were many pecks from many directions over an extended period. And the target was the same person.

People can get caught up in mobbing, but most people don't intentionally abuse someone. That is why awareness is so important and why paying attention to what is happening, really happening, is the key to prevention.

Most people who participate in mobbing, whether students or adults, often do so inadvertently. They don't understand the pain that they cause, how deeply it affects the target, or the long-range consequences.

Of course, there will always be some who are vicious and understand exactly what they are doing and get some sort of thrill or warped satisfaction from the suffering of another. These people need help also, for their sadistic tendencies, if left unrecognized and untreated, will affect them and others for a lifetime.

MYTHS ABOUT SCHOOL VIOLENCE

Robert C. DiGiulio

When it comes to the hot-button issue of school violence, separating fact from fiction in media reports can be difficult. Robert C. DiGiulio argues that it is essential to distinguish the myths from the actual evidence about school violence in order to understand and improve the problem. In this excerpt from his book *Educate, Medicate, or Litigate? What Teachers, Parents, and Administrators Must Do About Student Behavior*, he examines ten persistent myths that tend to skew public perception, such as the fallacy that schools are unsafe places for children. He also summarizes recent research and statistical evidence that provide a more accurate picture of school violence in the United States. DiGiulio is an education professor at Johnson State College in Johnson, Vermont, and the author of *Positive Classroom Management: A Step-by-Step Guide to Successfully Running the Show Without Destroying Student Dignity.*

I would like to address myths about schools and violence, myths that are particularly pernicious, standing in the way of realizing the great potential schools hold for improving the lives of millions throughout the world.

Ten Persistent Myths About Schools and Violence

Myth # 1: Schools Are Violent, Unsafe Places.

Reality. Contrary to the image of schools as violent places, schools have traditionally been—and remain—*the safest of places in the world* for children and adolescents. Schools are also among the safest of workplaces for adults who are employed in them. In comparable years (1992 and 1993), a total of 76 students were murdered or committed suicide at school—an average of about 38 each year. (*At school* includes in school, on school property, on the way to or from school, and while attending or traveling to or from school-sponsored events.) Six years later, a total of 69 students suffered school-associated, violent deaths (murder and suicide) in a 2-year period. The number also decreased 40% from 1998 to 1999, from 43 to 26.

Robert C. DiGiulio, *Educate, Medicate, or Litigate? What Teachers, Parents, and Administrators Must Do About Student Behavior*. Thousand Oaks, CA: Corwin Press, Inc., 2001.

However, an even more dramatic (and relevant) comparison is found by examining the rate of murder outside school compared with the rate in school. Even looking at the years 1992–1993, when the number of in-school, violent deaths was highest for any 2-year period, young persons between the ages of 5 and 19 were *over 100 times more likely* to be murdered away from school than at school according to a report from the Office of Juvenile Justice and Delinquency Prevention. In other years, out-of-school, violent deaths outnumber in-school, violent deaths several hundredfold. By any measure, schools are safe havens from serious violence, particularly in neighborhoods that are relatively dangerous.

In America, the frequency of violence in schools is related to school size and location. According to principals' reports [recorded by the U.S. Department of Education in 1998], large schools (1,000 or more students) experience more than 3 times the incidence of violent behavior than small- and medium-sized schools. Violence is more likely to be reported in urban schools, compared with suburban and rural schools, although that difference has recently gotten smaller.

But perhaps the single most telling piece of evidence of the relative safety of schools comes from the insurance industry, experts in risk assessment. For kindergarten and Grades 1 to 12, student health insurance for bodily injury only, for the 2000–2001 school year, costs $16 for the Schooltime-Only Plan (covering bodily injury "while attending school when school is in session"). The Around-the-Clock Plan (covering bodily injury "at home, school or away . . . or just playing in the neighborhood") costs $62 per school year. Subtracting 7 hours for sleeping and subtracting $16 for the 7 hours of school, this latter coverage costs $46 for the 10-hour, nonschool period or $4.60 per hour for out-of-school coverage, compared with $2.28 per hour for in-school–only coverage. In other words, judging by the cost of insurance, the risk of bodily injury is more than twice as high out of school as in school.

The Extent of School Violence

Myth #2: School Violence Is Increasing.

Reality. It is declining. Data from the Youth Risk Behavior Surveys were analyzed as to the numbers of students in high school grades who engaged in violent behaviors. In almost every category, the number of violent behaviors has decreased. In the period between 1991 and 1997, students involved in a physical fight decreased 14% from 42.5 to 36.6, the percentage of students injured in a fight decreased 20%, and the percentage of students who carried a weapon decreased by 30%. The researchers found each of these decreases to be statistically significant. They concluded by stating that these school-related declines between 1991 and 1997 parallel declines in homicide, nonfatal victimization, and other school crime rates.

Paradoxically, the American public believes that school violence is rising. Telephone polls conducted for *The Wall Street Journal* and for *NBC News* revealed that 71% of Americans surveyed thought a school shooting was likely to happen in their community, and 60% of those polled 7 months after the Columbine High School tragedy were worried a great deal about school violence. Interestingly, "polls showed that rural parents were most fearful of school violence, even though the overwhelming majority of serious crime against or by youth occurs in cities," [in the words of researchers K. Brooks, V. Schiraldi, and J. Ziedenberg].

Although the number of incidents of in-school violence is decreasing, the number of students suspended and expelled from schools has risen dramatically, almost doubling between 1974, when approximately 1.7 million students were suspended, and 1997, when 3.1 million students were suspended. Perhaps even more surprising is the reason for most school suspensions: They are for nonviolent causes, led by truancy, then tardiness. Fighting is third, followed by noncompliance with school policies. Similar to patterns seen in imprisonment rates, school suspensions fall disproportionately on male students and, in particular, on black male students, who are suspended at more than twice the rate of white students nationally, according to Norma Cantu, Assistant Secretary of Education for Civil Rights.

Although the school violence statistics show a decreasing rate, statistics do not give a complete picture of antisocial behavior in schools. Over the past 30 years, the amount of incivility and lower-level, serious antisocial behavior has probably increased, and according to some educators and observers, increased dramatically. Anecdotal reports from teachers, administrators, and others who work with children and adolescents describe an increase in rudeness and harsh interpersonal behavior including "dissing," vulgar language, and what a teacher friend of mine refers to as "name-calling, eye-rolling, in-your-face behavior" directed at peers and adults. Incivility is more difficult to measure than violent crime: It's simple to count the number of arrests, injuries, and deaths but tough to quantify a climate of incivility. But as a guess, I would point to the dramatically increased number of school suspensions (which are mostly for nonviolent offenses) as a sign of the increase in incivility: Students with a negative or hostile attitude are probably more likely to be suspended than cooperative, prosocial students. It may, therefore, follow that principals are given just the grounds they need to suspend a student when the hostile student is truant or tardy or becomes involved in a fight.

Violent Crime in America

Myth 3: Americans Are No More or Less Violent than Anyone Else.

Reality. Although schools are not the usual sites of violence or homicide in America, America does have a high rate of homicide compared with the rest of the world. U.S. children are 5 times more likely to be murdered than children in other industrialized countries. According to the Centers for Disease Control and Prevention, the United States had the highest rates of childhood homicide, suicide, and firearm-related deaths of 26 countries they studied. The greatest discrepancy between the United States and other industrialized nations, however, was in the proportion of firearm-related deaths of young persons, with the U.S. rates 12 times higher than rates in other industrialized nations. But even if we were to exclude firearm-related homicides, the remaining number of homicides of American children is almost 4 times other countries' rates. Nonetheless, the vast majority of these homicides do not occur in school, at school-sponsored events, or on school property. Child homicides in the United States occur almost exclusively outside of and away from school.

Returning to the question of crime in America, it must be emphasized that most crime in America is nonviolent. Only 1 of every 10 persons arrested in the United States is arrested for a violent crime, and only 3% of all arrests are for a crime that has resulted in some form of bodily injury. The prison-school parallel is worthy of note: The vast majority of prisoners are serving prison time for nonviolent offenses, and the vast majority of suspended and expelled students have been put out of school due mostly to nonviolent offenses of truancy and tardiness. (Recently, the city of Detroit has melded the two penalties: Parents have been sent to prison when their children have been truant from school.)

Is America more violent than other nations? If the percentage of imprisoned people is the measure, then yes, Americans are more violent. But given the many paths to prison in America, violence is hard to pin down outside of crime and homicide figures, which themselves should be seen with caution, for crimes and homicides are defined differently in other nations. Violence may not come to the attention of reporting agencies in other nations as efficiently as it does in America and in American schools.

Violence Rates Among Young People

Myth #4: Young People Are Becoming More Violent.

Reality. Although the U.S. rates of juvenile crime are high compared with other industrialized nations, those rates for violent crimes are falling. Data from the FBI's *Uniform Crime Reports* show a 56% decline in juvenile homicide from 1993 to 1998, with a 30% decline in the overall rate of juvenile crime. The American Medical Association recently reported an analysis of data from 1991–1997 Youth Risk Behavior Surveys, which revealed that between 1991 and 1997, U.S. high school students became less likely to carry weapons, to engage in physical fights, and to be injured in physical fights.

This is a very surprising piece of information, given the fact that, first, almost all young children's homicides are gun related, and second, the estimated number of guns available to adolescents is perceived to have grown exponentially since the 1960s. In fact, the overall rate of adult and juvenile crime has been falling. In 2000, the FBI revealed that both violent crimes and property crimes had decreased nationwide by 7%, representing the eighth consecutive year that reported crime had fallen. Yet the answer to the question "Are young people becoming more violent?" winds up hinging on how we define *young people*, for although juvenile crime rates (crimes committed by youths under 18 years of age) are falling, the crime rate of young male adults (those 18 years to 30 years of age) has risen fairly sharply.

Myth #5: Younger Children Are Committing More Murders.

Reality. The murder rate has fallen. More precisely, the arrest rate of children has decreased: The rate of children younger than 13 years of age arrested for murder fell from .20 per million in 1964 to .11 per million in 1998 (22 children under the age of 13 were arrested for murder in 1998). Over that same 34-year period, the number of youths younger than 18 years of age arrested for any juvenile crime dropped by 30%, with rates for rape falling 29%, robbery decreasing 47%, and aggravated assault falling 27%. However, there is no clear answer to this question, because there are variables, such as changes in the way children are charged (murder, homicide, involuntary manslaughter, etc.) and changes in the legal resources available between 1964 and 1998 (for example, the number of lawyers in America has risen significantly in that period). Thus we cannot conclude that younger and younger children are more likely—or less likely—to kill today than in years past. We simply don't know.

Myth #6: Older Students Are More Likely to Be Victims than Younger Students.

Reality. Young adolescents are more frequently victims of violence than older adolescents or younger children. Although schools are safe places, when they are unsafe, they are unsafe mostly for young adolescents. There is an uptick in the rates of violence around ages 11, 12, and 13. Violent victimization appears to peak at age 12, which is a time of physical transition (puberty) as well as educational transition (moving on to middle school). In both 1989 and 1995, students at age 12 were about 3 times more likely to be victims of violence than students at age 17 and 18. This is due in part, of course, to the fact that students who drop out of school tend to do so after age 16; those 17- and 18-year-olds who remain in school are generally not predisposed toward violent behavior. On the other hand, those age 16 and older who drop out are significantly more likely to be involved in a physical fight and carry a weapon. Adolescents who are not enrolled in school are also much more likely to smoke cigarettes and to use alcohol or other illegal drugs. The value of school as a safe place is shown quite dramatically by such statistics.

Harsh Measures

Myth #7: The Only Effective Way to Stop Violence Is Through Punitive Measures.

Reality. This is a persistent and dangerous myth that breeds much violence in itself. There is no evidence that harsh measures, such as suspension, expulsion, and incarceration, have any long-term and immediate effect on reducing antisocial or violent behavior in either in-school or non-school-related populations. Of course, expulsion, suspension, or incarceration brings relief to a school or classroom in which the offenders are removed. However, such measures simply relocate the problem: to the streets, to the mall, to the community, to the prisons. Police organizations do not tend to support zero-tolerance measures, for they know quite well where suspended and expelled students go and what they do when they are banned from school. Once a student has been put out of school, that student will be at a significantly higher risk for arrest, drug and alcohol use, and ultimately, premature death. Unfortunately, the political system cannot or will not take a look at the big picture involved with suspensions and expulsions, and this denial is worsening: Florida governor Jeb Bush signed into law a bill that exempted Florida schools from having the number of students suspended or expelled included in their school-accountability measures. Starting July 1, 2000, Florida schools could move toward their "excellence bonuses," as they were freed to suspend and expel as many students as they wished without accountability.

This does not mean that students with behavior disorders or violent students, in Florida or anywhere else, should remain and disrupt classes. But there are many alternatives to expulsion and suspension, alternatives that change negative behavior rather than pushing it out of view. For instance, research shows that teaching young people alternatives to violence works to prevent violence and has many other constructive side effects. In addition, teaching young people peaceful ways to respond to conflict has longer-term benefits; it can carry over into adulthood. Teaching about nonviolence and peace serves to increase prosocial behavior, reduces physical aggression, and has even been connected with improved academic achievement. The only disadvantages of the use of educational measures to prevent violence involve time and image: Education is never a quick fix, and educative measures never appear to be as tough looking as expulsion, suspension, and incarceration. As a result, even *educational measures we know to be successful* are not likely to be advocated by politicians seeking to portray an I'm-tough-on-crime image.

Myth #8: Schools Are More Dangerous for Girls.

Reality. Boys are more often the initiators of serious antisocial behavior, and boys are more likely to be the victims of violence in school. In 1989 and 1995, about twice as many boys as girls between 12 and 18 years of age reported violent victimization at school, with female students about one fourth as likely to be murdered at school as male students. (Violent victimization included physical attacks or taking property directly from the student with force, weapons, or threats.) According to the Centers for Disease Control and Prevention, male students are also more likely to have carried a weapon on school property, and males are more likely to have been threatened or injured by a weapon on school property. Males constituted 83% of all victims of school-related homicides or suicides. Criminal justice professor Daniel Lockwood looked at violence in middle schools and high schools, finding that violence involved more boys than girls, yet "the average number of incidents per student was about the same" for boys as for girls. He found that "boys tended to fight mainly with other boys," but "girls were involved in almost as many fights with boys as with other girls." Curiously, "girls were the offenders in all incidents in which knives were used."

Girls may feel less safe in school than boys, although a 1998 survey of 20,000 students revealed the levels of *feeling unsafe* to be similar between high school males and females. More dramatic than gender differences, however, are racial-plus-gender differences, with black males far more likely than any other group to be victims of murder as well as victims of other forms of violent behavior inside and outside of school.

Visible Signs of Security

Myth #9: Security Measures Such as Guards, Metal Detectors, and Video Cameras Make Schools Safer.

Reality. Researchers are saying the opposite may be true. Although it is too soon to draw definite conclusions, visible signs of security along with zero-tolerance policies appear to make students feel less safe. Even as the number of weapons brought to school and confiscated at school continues to drop, today's students feel less safe than ever before. Almost all American schools now restrict access to their buildings; 11% have either a security guard or metal detectors in addition to restricted access; and 3% of all schools have restricted access, a full-time security guard, and metal detector checkpoints. Nonetheless, a recent series of surveys conducted by the Horatio Alger Association of Distinguished Americans found that the number of public school students who said they always feel safe at school dropped from 44% in 1998 to 37% in 1999. The enforced wearing by students and staff of identification cards or badges has raised opposition from student groups and civil-liberties organizations. In several states, students have reacted in strong opposition to the badges that display their name and usually their photograph and sometimes their Social Security numbers.

Education professor Anne Westcott Dodd asks

How much will video cameras and police patrols help when a student feels like an outsider . . . when a student who typically responds to school authorities with hostility feels like a prison inmate as he enters the school each day?

Moreover, the nonhostile student will also feel threatened or unsettled by visible signs of security. Professor Dodd concludes that "locked doors and uniformed officers may make the school more secure but will probably do little to make individual students feel safe."

Long-Term Outcomes

Myth #10: Aggressive Children Usually Turn Out Just Fine as Adults.

Reality. They usually do not, and this is one of the clearest findings we have as well as one of the outcomes we can do much more to prevent. Aggressive behavior by a young child is one of the surest predictors of criminality at age 18. In a study of aggressive behavior over time, children were observed on multiple occasions interacting with a familiar peer at age 2. They were then observed again 3 years later. The researchers found that high levels of aggression and dependency at age 2 were significant predictors of antisocial behavior at age 6. They found that problematic behaviors were both more frequent and more stable over time for boys than for girls.

Patricia Chamberlain, director of parenting and foster care programs for the Oregon Social Learning Center, said that intervention must begin at an early age: "We know that if a child is being aggressive in the first grade, they're not likely to grow out of it." The Center began a study in 1983 to assess the role of parenting on children's behavior and to see, later on in life, what effect early behavior has on later development. The children-subjects are now in their twenties, and the results are dramatic: Of those children with behavior problems in the fourth grade (including fighting, stealing, or lying), almost half had been arrested by age 14. Within that group of children with early arrest records, 75% were repeatedly arrested at least three times by the time they reached 18 years of age. Dan Olweus's extensive international research into bullying clearly shows that bullying behavior starts early, and unless there are systematic efforts to change that behavior, bullying behavior persists rather strongly. Olweus found that "35% to 40% of boys who were characterized as bullies in Grades 6 through 9 had been convicted of at least three officially registered crimes by the age of 24," but this was the case with only 10% of boys who were not identified as bullies in Grades 6 through 9. If there is one area that begs early intervention, it is this.

From Myth to Reality

Myths about schools and violence persist despite, in many cases, an abundance of countervailing evidence. Having entered the new century, we appear to have come to the time when we should move away from myths and move away from measures that do little or nothing to reduce antisocial and violent behavior. Threatening children and adolescents with imprisonment and with suspension from school is ineffective, particularly for those at whom such strong measures are directed. Although most world cultures hold that it is a parent's responsibility to teach children prosocial behavior, blaming parents when they fail is a futile pursuit. Similarly, we should hold schools accountable; yet viewing schools as sources of violence or blaming schools for the escalation of violent behavior is counterproductive, because schools hold the greatest potential of any public or private institutions for providing a solution. It is time to refocus on what we know about children and children's behavior and about how children are socialized. For several thousand years, children have learned prosocial behavior from those around them, not from abstract, written laws and litigation, and not from sedative medication. This refocus on socialization is within our capability, for we have today reached a point at which we have an absolute abundance of both anecdotal and research information in the fields of behavioral medicine, sociology, psychology, education, and human development.

CHAPTER 2

THE CAUSES OF SCHOOL VIOLENCE

RISK FACTORS FOR VIOLENT STUDENT BEHAVIOR

Kimberly M. Williams

Research has identified several risk factors that may contribute to the likelihood that a student will become violent, Kimberly M. Williams states in the following excerpt from her book *The Peace Approach to Violence Prevention: A Guide for Administrators and Teachers*. These risk factors include maltreatment by parents, exposure to violence in the family or neighborhood, poor school performance, and depression. Williams explains that teachers and administrators can utilize these warning signs to identify students in need of help. The risk factors should never be used to label, exclude, or punish students, she asserts; rather, they should be used to determine appropriate services for these students. Williams directs the evaluation for the Safe Schools, Healthy Students project for the Syracuse City School District in New York. She is also a professor in the school of education at the State University of New York at Cortland.

Both formal and informal strategies help identify students at risk of violent behavior. Early identification is critical to prevention. However, a word of caution: just because a student is identified as "at risk," he or she should not be ostracized or victimized. Students in need of support services should receive them. Creating a plan that involves the student (once identified), his or her family, and a caseworker, social worker, counselor, or special educator must also be a part of any plan. In addition, research literature has demonstrated that risk factors may be poor predictors of future violence. The following section summarizes some of the research findings on risk factors as well as warning signs of psychological problems that are sometimes associated with violent behaviors in schools and signs of other underreported forms of violence.

The Office of Juvenile Justice and Delinquency Prevention commissioned a report in 2000 that broke down risk factors by individual factors, family factors, school factors, peer-related factors, and community and neighborhood factors. They examined the research literature on youth violence in an attempt to identify some factors that put children at risk of violent and destructive criminal behavior. In this comprehensive report, they identified the following risk factors.

Individual factors:
- Pregnancy and delivery complications when the student was born
- Low resting heart rate
- Internalizing disorders (nervousness, withdrawal, worrying, and anxiety)
- Hyperactivity, concentration problems, restlessness, and risk taking
- Aggressiveness
- Early initiation of violent behavior
- Involvement in other forms of antisocial behavior
- Beliefs and attitudes favorable to deviant or antisocial behavior

Family factors:
- Parent criminality
- Child maltreatment
- Poor family management practices
- Low levels of parental involvement
- Poor family bonding and family conflict
- Parental attitudes favorable to substance abuse and violence
- Parent-child separation

School factors:
- Academic failure
- Low bonding to school
- Truancy and dropping out of school
- Frequent school transitions

Peer-related factors:
- Delinquent siblings
- Delinquent peers
- Gang membership

Community and neighborhood factors:
- Poverty
- Community disorganization
- Availability of drugs and firearms
- Neighborhood adults involved in crime
- Exposure to violence and racial prejudice

These risk factors have been associated with violence in schools, although all are not created equal. This list should not be used as a checklist where children with more of these risk factors are at higher risk for violence than those with none. . . .

The American Psychological Association's Risk Factors

The American Psychological Association (APA) offered the following risk factors to help educators identify youth at risk of violence:

- A history of violent or aggressive behavior
- Serious drug or alcohol use
- Gang membership or strong desire to be in a gang
- Access to or fascination with weapons, especially guns
- Threatening others
- Regular trouble controlling feelings like anger, or withdrawal from friends and usual activities
- Feeling rejected or alone
- Having been a victim of bullying
- Poor school performance
- History of discipline problems or frequent run-ins with authority
- Feeling constantly disrespected
- Failing to acknowledge the feelings or rights of others

American Academy of Child and Adolescent Psychiatry's Warning Signs

According to the American Academy of Child and Adolescent Psychiatry, there are different psychological classifications used in schools to classify children with aggressive behaviors or a group of other problem behaviors. Table 1 describes three classifications that may be associated with violent behavior in schools: oppositional defiant disorder (ODD), conduct disorder (CD), and antisocial personality disorder.

In addition to these three classifications, there is another classification for aggressive youth used in schools: emotional disturbance (ED). Special educators typically use this term to classify students who have chronic emotional conditions that interfere with their ability to participate in the traditional educational system. These students typically have behavioral and social interactions that are developmentally behind and make concentrating and functioning in the more typical classroom challenging.

Conduct disorder, oppositional defiance, antisocial personality, and emotional disturbance include problem behaviors that are more obviously associated with youth at risk of violence in schools. In addition to these more overt behaviors, we need to examine those behaviors that may be less obvious, but can be just as troubling and problematic.

Risk Factors for More Concealed Psychological Classifications

Other psychological classifications are associated with children at risk of violence but their behaviors may be somewhat more concealed (quiet, sad, or withdrawn) than those described in Table 1—including the often-omitted forms of violence to the self as well as grief and depression. The following will be discussed briefly here: posttraumatic stress disorder, grief, depression, self-mutilation, and suicide.

Posttraumatic stress disorder. One psychological classification that might be present among at-risk youth is posttraumatic stress disorder (PTSD). Children with PTSD may show the following symptoms (reprinted from American Academy of Child and Adolescent Psychiatry):

- Worry about dying at an early age
- Losing interest in activities
- Having physical symptoms such as headaches and stomachaches
- Showing more sudden and extreme emotional reactions
- Having problems falling or staying asleep
- Showing irritability or angry outbursts
- Having problems concentrating

Table 1. American Academy of Child and Adolescent Psychiatry: Labels of Psychological Classifications for Childhood Aggressive Disorders

Oppositional Defiant Disorder	Conduct Disorder	Antisocial Personal Disorder
Loses temper	Aggression to people, animals	Evidence of conduct disorder prior to age 15
Argues with adults	Bullies, threatens, intimidates, uses dangerous weapons, physically cruel to people and animals, forced into sex	Failure to conform to social norms
Refuses adult requests	Destruction of property	Deceitfulness
Does things to annoy	Fire setting	Impulsivity
Blames other for own mistakes	Stealing with confrontation	Irritability
Touchy, easily annoyed, angry, resentful	Deliberate destruction of property	Physical aggression
Spiteful, vindictive, vengeful	Theft and serious violation of rules	Reckless disregard for safety of others
Initiates confrontation—more likely with adults and others the child knows well	Steals, lies, runs away, truant, serious and consistent violation of rules	Consistent irresponsibility, lack of remorse
Onset before age 8 to early adolescence	Six-month duration; onset usually prepuberty	Classification at 18 years; usually has label of ODD and CD
Childhood/adolescence 2–16% of the population	Childhood/adolescence 2–16% male 2–9% female	Adulthood 3% males 1% females

- Acting younger than their age (e.g., clingy or whiny behavior, thumb sucking)
- Showing increased alertness to the environment
- Repeating behavior that reminds them of the trauma

Children who are victims of violence are at high risk of becoming perpetrators of violence. These same children may likely experience PTSD as a result of the violence they have experienced.

Grief and loss. In addition, many children in high-risk neighborhoods experience a great deal of loss in their lives (death of loved ones, friends, family, etc.) and have no outlet for their grief. Children [in one study of a high-risk neighborhood], for example, missed a lot of school to attend funerals and wakes for loved ones. They witnessed death on the streets and in their homes, some on a fairly regular basis, with no opportunities for psychological help to deal with their grief. The American Academy of Child and Adolescent Psychiatry listed the following signs of a child having difficulty with loss:

- An extended period of depression in which the child loses interest in daily activities and events
- Inability to sleep, loss of appetite, prolonged fear of being alone
- Acting much younger for an extended period
- Excessively imitating the dead person
- Repeated statements of wanting to join the dead person
- Withdrawal from friends
- Sharp drop in school performance or refusal to attend school

Some students who experience a great deal of loss may hide these feelings. If you know that a student has experienced a loss or frequent loss, it is important to consider that the child might need help dealing with his or her grief.

Depression. The American Academy of Child and Adolescent Psychiatry identified the following warning signs for depression:

- Frequent sadness, tearfulness, crying
- Hopelessness
- Decreased interest in activities or an inability to enjoy previously favorite activities
- Persistent boredom, low energy
- Social isolation, poor communication
- Low self-esteem and guilt
- Extreme sensitivity to rejection or failure
- Increased irritability, anger, or hostility
- Difficulty with relationships
- Frequent complaints of physical illnesses such as headaches and stomachaches
- Frequent absences from school or poor performance in school
- Poor concentration
- A major change in eating or sleeping patterns
- Talk of or efforts to run away from home

- Thoughts or expressions of suicide or self-destructive behavior

Children with warning signs of depression are also at risk of violence against themselves or others. Children feeling chronic despair or depression may feel as though they have nothing to lose by acting out any aggressive fantasies. Psychological help should be made available to students showing consistent signs of depression.

Risk Factors for Harming Oneself

Depending on your own personal definition of violence (whether or not it includes harm to the self), you may not think about such behaviors as suicide and self-mutilation when thinking about violence. However, these forms of violence turned inward are very significant, harmful, and lethal types of violence that need to be considered in our discussions of violence and our examination of risk factors that students display.

Suicide. Suicide is a tragedy that affects many young people, their family, and other loved ones. Threats of suicide should be taken very seriously to determine the severity of the threat. It is important to determine if the child making the threat has the means to commit suicide. It is important to seek professional psychological help immediately when a child makes threats of suicide. The American Academy of Child and Adolescent Psychiatry offers the following signs or risk factors for youth at risk of committing suicide:

- Change in eating and sleeping habits
- Withdrawal from friends, family, and regular activities
- Violent actions, rebellious behavior, or running away
- Drug and alcohol use
- Unusual neglect of personal appearance
- Marked personality change
- Persistent boredom, difficulty concentrating, or a decline in the quality of schoolwork
- Frequent complaints about physical symptoms, often related to emotions, such as stomachaches, headaches, fatigue, etc.
- Loss of interest in pleasurable activities
- Not tolerating praise or rewards

A teenager who is planning to commit suicide may also:
- Complain of being a bad person or feeling "rotten inside"
- Give verbal hints with statements such as, "I won't be a problem for you much longer," "Nothing matters," "It no use," and "I won't see you again."
- Put his or her affairs in order; for example, give away favorite possessions, clean his or her room, throw away important belongings, etc.
- Become suddenly cheerful after a period of depression
- Have signs of psychosis (hallucinations or bizarre thoughts)

If a child or adolescent says, "I want to kill myself" or "I'm going to commit suicide," always take the statement seriously and seek evaluation from a child and adolescent psychiatrist or other physician. People often feel uncomfortable talking about death. However, asking the child or adolescent whether he or she is depressed or thinking about suicide can be helpful. Rather than "putting thoughts in the child's head," such a question will provide assurance that somebody cares and will give the young person the chance to talk about problems.

Self-mutilation. Self-mutilation (sometimes referred to as self-injury) includes behaviors that are physically harmful or damaging to oneself (biting, carving, burning, hitting, bruising, etc.). These behaviors may be symptomatic of other psychological illnesses, but may be a way for children to deal with stress, anger, frustration, or low self-esteem. . . .

Teachers and administrators need to be on the lookout for these less overt warning signs of forms of violence (PTSD, grief, depression, etc.) as well as remaining vigilant for more overt warning signs of the other psychological classifications described (conduct disorder, oppositional defiance, etc.). Immediate referral to appropriate mental health staff in schools or outside agencies is critical. It is important to remember that school psychologists and special educators are experts in identifying all of the behaviors listed above and in helping students receive appropriate services. Work with a team of psychological specialists to make sure that students receive appropriate services, and follow up with the service providers as well as the student and his or her family to make sure that the assistance is making a positive difference.

A Word of Caution About Risk Factors

Risk factors have been shown to be ineffective and inappropriate to predict future violent behavior of children—resulting in many children being inappropriately labeled. Be careful that you never use these risk factors to label, exclude, stereotype, or punish a child but rather consider these factors as a part of a whole context including a child, family, school, and larger community. Risk factors might be used to identify appropriate services for students. One risk factor, or even a couple, does not mean a student will be violent. These risk factors should be taken within the whole-school context and as a part of the student within that context. These are not absolute predictors of violent behavior, so please be careful with their use. . . .

Protective Factors

Any discussion of risk factors and warning signs must include a reflection on protective factors. Protective factors may buffer risk factors from having a negative impact on a child. Teachers and administrators can use information on risk factors to identify student needs and assess the ability of programs or program components to address these needs. However, it is also important to identify protective factors that promote successful development.

Three key factors that have been identified as fostering the development of resiliency:

1. Caring and support (e.g., creating caring, cooperative classrooms, mentoring opportunities)
2. High expectations (e.g., having high expectations of student performance in your classrooms)
3. Opportunities for meaningful participation and a sense of bonding to the school (e.g., helping students feel a part of the classroom community, participating in cocurricular and classroom activities)

D.J. Hawkins, R.F. Catalano, and J. Miller identified the following protective factors that reduce a student's risk of substance abuse that may also place students at risk of school violence:

1. Individual characteristics: Some students have more resilient temperaments—accepting disappointment well and not letting themselves get hurt easily. These children are the ones who seem to adapt to challenging situations. Students who have positive peers and positive role models are also at reduced risk.
2. Bonding: Students with strong positive bonds to and relationships with their families, friends, school, and community are at lower risk. These students tend to set and work to achieve goals valued by those with whom they have positive relationships. School has a role in helping them achieve their goals. Students with constant school failure often create goals that they feel do not include academic success (e.g., dancer, rap musician, homemaker, professional athlete). These students often do not feel bonded to school because of academic failure that began early in their school careers. Getting children bonded and able to see the important role of school in their futures is important to building resiliency.
3. Healthy beliefs and clear standards: Students who have schools, families, or peers who teach them healthy beliefs and enforce clear standard for behavior, such as being drug free, eating healthfully, exercising and taking care of one's body, being community oriented, respectful of others, focused on learning, and being strong academically, will be at reduced risk for violence.

What School Personnel Can Do

The previously listed behaviors demonstrate behaviors that have been associated with students being put at risk of violent behavior as well as factors that have been found to protect students against these risk factors. As teachers or administrators, you should be prepared to:

- Thoughtfully and carefully recognize these at-risk behaviors as a tool for getting help or services for youth who could best benefit from services.
- Work to build a caring climate in classrooms and the school as a whole.

- Address and make clear that cruel treatment, including the use of put-downs and ostracizing or purposefully leaving other students out during work and play, is not tolerated. Students need to be encouraged to include all of their peers in kind ways. Preventing these low levels of aggression or precursors to more dangerous forms of violence will help prevent students becoming at greater risk.
- Work to build protective factors for students at high risk, including helping all students develop healthy bonds with school, and have healthy beliefs and clear standards in and about school.
- Create caring, mentoring relationships with all students and be poised to get special help for students at risk.
- Involve at-risk students in the school through cocurricular and academic activities (tutoring, school programs, etc.).
- Build academic skills of all students with careful focus on early literacy skills. Literacy is the foundation of academic success. Many at-risk students need to build their basic literacy or other academic skills, but are reluctant to admit needing help.
- Be on the lookout for bullying (direct and indirect), sexual harassment, child abuse, relational aggression, and relationship/dating violence.

Easy Access to Guns Contributes to School Violence

Centers for Disease Control and Prevention

The Centers for Disease Control and Prevention (CDC) is the leading federal agency dedicated to promoting the health and safety of American citizens. In the following selection, the CDC summarizes the results of a seven-year study that examined the source of firearms used by students who committed murder or suicide in or near school grounds. According to the CDC, the study found that most of the students had obtained the guns from their homes, from friends, or from relatives. These findings reveal that adults need to become more aware of the importance of decreasing teens' unsupervised access to firearms and should make a greater effort to store guns safely whenever teenagers are present in the home.

During July 1, 1992–June 30, 1999, a total of 323 school-associated violent death events occurred in the United States, resulting in 358 deaths. To guide prevention efforts, the CDC [Centers for Disease Control and Prevention] examined school-associated firearm violent death events committed by students in elementary and secondary schools in the United States and determined the sources of the firearms used in these events. The findings indicate that, among the incidents for which data are available, the majority of the firearms used in these events were obtained from perpetrators' homes or from friends or relatives. The safe storage of firearms is critically important and should be continued. In addition, other strategies that might prevent firearm-related injuries and deaths among students, such as safety and design changes for firearms, should be evaluated.

A Seven-Year Study

A school-associated violent death event was defined as a firearm-related homicide or suicide in which the homicide perpetrator or the suicide victim was an elementary or secondary school student and the fatal injury occurred during July 1, 1992–June 30, 1999, either 1) on

Centers for Disease Control and Prevention, "Source of Firearms Used in School-Associated Violent Deaths," *Morbidity and Mortality Weekly Report*, March 7, 2003, pp. 169–72.

the campus of a functioning public or private elementary or secondary school in the United States, 2) while the victim was on the way to or from regular sessions at such a school, or 3) while the victim was attending or traveling to or from an official school-sponsored event. Cases of school-associated violent deaths were identified through a systematic search of two computerized newspaper and broadcast media databases (Lexis-Nexis and Dialog). Data on the types of weapons used and their sources were collected through interviews with school and police officials and by reviewing official police reports. A perpetrator was defined as a student who committed either a homicide or suicide. Firearms used by perpetrators who committed a homicide and then killed themselves (i.e., a homicide-suicide event) were included in analyses of firearms used by homicide perpetrators.

During July 1, 1992–June 30, 1999, a total of 218 student perpetrators were involved directly in a school-associated homicide or suicide; 123 (56.4%) of these persons used at least one firearm at the time of the event. Among the student perpetrators who were carrying a firearm at the time of the event, 33 (26.8%) committed suicide, 85 (69.1%) perpetrated a homicide, and five (4.1%) perpetrated a homicide-suicide. The majority of these student perpetrators were male (93.5%). The median age of student perpetrators was 16 years (range: 10–21 years). Of the 90 homicide perpetrators (homicide and homicide-suicide combined), 14 (15.6%) participated in a multiple-victim homicide event, and 76 (84.4%) participated in a single-victim homicide event. One student committed suicide as part of a multiple-victim suicide event.

Five student perpetrators were carrying two firearms each, resulting in a total of 128 firearms used in these events. Of the 128 firearms, 48 (37.5%) came from the perpetrator's home, and 30 (23.4%) came from a friend or relative of the perpetrator; 26 (76.5%) of the firearms used by a student to commit suicide came from the home of the student, and 48 (51.0%) of the firearms used in homicide events came from the home (23.4%) or from a friend or relative (27.6%) of the homicide perpetrator. The source of 29 (22.7%) firearms used by student perpetrators was unknown.

Firearms used by students who committed a school-associated suicide were approximately 11 times more likely to come from their home than firearms used by students who committed homicide. Multiple-victim events were more likely to involve firearms from the home than single-victim events. Firearms from the home were used more often by female perpetrators than male perpetrators, and by non-Hispanic white perpetrators than perpetrators from other racial/ethnic groups. Perpetrators from two-parent families were four times more likely to use a firearm obtained from their home than perpetrators from single-parent/caretaker families. In addition, firearms used by perpetrators with no criminal history and perpetrators with no previous gang involvement were more likely to come from home than the firearms used by perpetrators who were members of a gang or had a criminal history. . . .

Prevention Strategies

Prevention strategies to reduce firearm homicides and suicides among children and youth typically involve both behavior-oriented and product-oriented approaches. Behavior-oriented approaches (e.g., firearm-safety counseling and child-access prevention laws for parents and firearm-avoidance and firearm-safety programs for children) rarely have been evaluated, and those that have been evaluated have shown limited effectiveness in reducing firearm violence.

One behavior-oriented approach in reducing firearm violence is firearm-safety counseling by pediatric health-care providers. Pediatric providers have been encouraged to counsel parents on the risks for having firearms in the home and the need to store them securely. Typical recommendations include storing firearms unloaded and locked with a trigger lock or in a locked firearm safe or portable locked handgun box. However, counseling alone might not be effective in preventing firearm homicides and suicides among children and youth. This might be because male parents, who are more likely to own firearms and know how they are stored than female parents, are less likely to bring their children to the pediatrician's office. Even when they are aware of a firearm in the home, parents with teenaged children are less likely to store firearms safely than parents with younger children, despite the fact that older children are at greater risk for firearm death.

The results of this study also indicate that it is not enough for parents to eliminate unsupervised access to firearms in their home; approximately 25% of the firearms used in school-associated homicides were obtained from friends or relatives. Parents should consider discussing access to firearms and safe-storage practices with their relatives and the parents of their children's friends.

The findings in this report are subject to at least four limitations. First, because events were identified from news media reports, any event not reported in the media was excluded. Second, this report includes events associated with schools; other homicide and suicide events involving school-aged perpetrators might have different firearm-acquisition patterns. Third, the results reported for homicide events might not reflect the true distribution of sources because the source of the firearms in approximately 25% of these events is unknown. Finally, among the student perpetrators who obtained their firearms from home or from friends or relatives, how the students gained access to these firearms is unknown.

Safety Features

The safe storage of firearms is critically important and should be continued. In addition to safe storage of firearms, changing the design of firearms might prevent firearm injuries among teenagers and younger children by making firearms more difficult to use unintentionally or intentionally if stolen or obtained illegally. Many safety features for firearms (e.g., grip safety mechanisms, loaded chamber indicators, and magazine disconnect devices) are intended to reduce unintentional firearm injuries. Emerging technologies (e.g., personalization of handguns) are designed to prevent unauthorized users of any age from firing a firearm and might reduce access to firearms by adolescents. Although changing product design has benefitted child-poisoning prevention efforts and motor-vehicle safety programs, the impact of product-oriented approaches in reducing youth firearm violence is unknown and requires evaluation. However, the findings in this report can assist parents, school personnel, and the community at large in developing and implementing prevention strategies to decrease school-associated firearm injuries.

Are Children with Special Needs More Likely to Commit School Violence?

Denise (Smith) Skarbek

Denise (Smith) Skarbek worked as a special education teacher for children with mild disabilities before becoming a professor in the department of special education at Indiana University at South Bend. Her interest in special education led her to research the relationship between children with special needs and school violence. In this selection, she explores whether children with certain emotional and cognitive disabilities are at greater risk for committing violent acts in school. As Skarbek writes, there is some evidence that suggests these children may be more likely to act out in aggressive or violent ways. On the other hand, she observes, none of the perpetrators in recent school shootings were identified as children with disabilities. Skarbek concludes that since the research findings are mixed, school personnel should avoid singling out children with disabilities as potential troublemakers.

The random acts of targeted school shootings of the past several years have prompted many scholars to search for explanations of *why* and question *who* is committing these horrific violent acts and whether additional attacks will occur. In fact, the U.S. Secret Service examined the thinking, planning, and other preattack behaviors engaged by attackers who carried out the school shootings to determine (a) whether the attacks were being planned, and, (b) if yes, what could have been done to prevent further attacks. The major findings reported were as follows:

- Incidents of targeted violence at school rarely were sudden, impulsive acts.
- Prior to most incidents, other people knew about the attacker's idea or plan to attack.
- There is no useful "profile" of students engaged in targeted school violence.
- Most attackers engaged in some behavior prior to the incident

that caused others concern or indicated a need for help.

- Most attackers had difficulty coping with significant losses or personal failures. Moreover, many had conspired or attempted suicide.
- Many attackers felt bullied, persecuted, or injured by others prior to the attack.
- Most attackers had access to and had weapons prior to the attack.
- In many cases, other students were involved in some capacity.
- Despite prompt law enforcement responses, most shooting incidents were stopped by means other than law enforcement intervention.

Other researchers have questioned the role, if any, children with disabilities played in any of the recent school-yard shootings, while others have considered the role special education legislation has played in school violence. . . .

Special Education Legislation and School Violence

Approximately 11 percent of school-age children between the ages of 6 and 17 are identified as receiving special education services in the United States. Public Law 105-17, the Individuals with Disabilities Act (IDEA), which is the reauthorization of P.L. 94-142 Education for All Handicapped Children Act, protects the educational interests of children with disabilities. Some believe that P.L. 105-17 prevents school violence whereas others believe that it promotes school violence.

According to IDEA, special education is "specifically designed instruction, at no cost to parents, to meet the unique needs of a child with a disability. . . . This includes instruction conducted in the classroom, home, hospitals and institutions, and in other settings and instruction in physical education." Two major provisions of IDEA include the right to free and appropriate education with nondisabled peers to the maximum extent appropriate or what has been referred to as the *least restrictive environment*. The key to providing a free and appropriate education is individualized instruction. To ensure that all children identified as having a disability receive individualized instruction, IDEA mandates that an individualized education program (IEP) be developed. In the development of this individualized program, the case conference committee considers the child's current level of educational performance and special needs, the services to be delivered, objectives to be met, timelines for completion, and assessment progress.

Perhaps the most controversial aspects of Public Law 105-17 are the discipline provisions, such as the "stay-put" rule and the cumulative ten-school-day limit on suspensions. Legislation mandates that a child with a disability remain in his or her current educational placement, pending the completion of any due-process proceedings, court proceedings, or appeals. Many argue that the stay-put provision of

IDEA promotes school violence because it unfairly protects students with disabilities who are disruptive or violent. They argue that the school's options are limited when there is a legitimate reason to remove a dangerous or extremely disruptive child.

Special Treatment?

Some school administrators and many members of Congress thought that the stay-put provision contributed to the excessive violence that has erupted in the schools during the past several years. For example, Congress was concerned that students with disabilities could bring guns to school and yet would not be expelled as would their nondisabled violent peers. Furthermore, it was believed that IDEA prevented school officials from disciplining and expelling students with disabilities with behavior problems: "even if a student with a disability commits a serious infraction of the rules, such as bringing a gun to school, he or she can only be suspended for 10 days as opposed to the mandatory one year expulsion handed to other students accused of the same crime," [in the words of W.J. Cahir]. According to Cahir "many school officials argue that IDEA creates a dangerous Catch 22. If a student's violent or antisocial behavior stems from a disability, the officials' disciplinary options become limited. Only when a child's education team determines that his misconduct is unrelated to his disability may the school discipline the student as it would others."

Cahir argues that students with a disability charged with weapons and drug-related offenses can be removed from their school and sent to an alternative placement for a maximum of forty-five calendar days. This, according to Cahir, is in direct contrast to the 1994 federal Gun-Free Schools Act, which requires that any nondisabled child who possesses a gun in school be expelled for at least one year: "Schools can also move a child with a disability to an alternative placement if a hearing officer determines the student poses a threat to himself or others—a litigious, appealable, time-consuming process."

Moreover, some school administrators and teachers raised concerns about their ability to maintain school safety and order and at the same time instruct students with disabilities. It was argued that when students with disabilities engaged in serious misconduct, they continued to receive educational services in schools because of the protections afforded by IDEA. In contrast, nondisabled students involved in similar misconduct were suspended or expelled without educational services.

The Intent of the Provision

In contrast, others believe that IDEA attempts to strike a balance between the need to provide a safe, orderly environment and the need to protect children with disabilities from unwarranted exclusion through disciplinary proceedings. To appreciate this controversy one must understand the intent of IDEA's stay-put provision and other provisions provided by special education legislation.

School personnel may suspend children with disabilities for up to ten school days at a time for separate incidents of misconduct to the extent that such action would be applied to nondisabled peers. Change in placement for more than ten consecutive school days constitutes a change in educational placement, which triggers several procedural safeguards. The IEP team must meet immediately to review the relationship between the child's disability and the behavior subject to disciplinary action. The IEP team takes into consideration several factors such as evaluation and diagnostic results, placement appropriateness, if the disability impaired the child's ability to understand the consequences of the behavior subject to discipline, and if the child's disability impaired his ability to control the behavior.

If the behavior was a result of the child's disability, the IEP team revisits the individualized program to determine what changes need to be implemented to address the child's behavior. [Z.H. Rudo, V. Robbins, and D. Smith] believe that the IEP is one way to decrease a child's violent behavior, especially since IDEA requires educators to conduct functional behavioral assessments and to implement behavior intervention plans that include positive behavioral interventions and supports. These mandates are aimed at providing students with disabilities, particularly those who are at risk for or who engage in aggressive and violent behavior, with the necessary skills to handle their anger and aggression in acceptable ways.

On the other hand, if the IEP team determines that the violent behavior was not a manifestation of the child's disability then disciplinary procedures used for nondisabled peers can be used with the child with a disability. On May 20, 1999, the Senate approved an amendment to Juvenile Justice Bill that changes the IDEA stay-put rule. This revision gives school officials the option of removing for one year a student with a disability who brings a bomb or gun to school. This revision contradicts the assumption that IDEA promotes school violence. In essence, IDEA acknowledges the importance of addressing behavioral problems for children with special needs and requires special educators to address identified behavioral problems.

[In 2001] the U.S. General Accounting Office (GAO) conducted a study to determine how the IDEA amendments of 1997 affected the ability of schools to maintain a safe environment conducive to learning. The results suggest that nondisabled students and students with disabilities are generally disciplined the same; for example, 60 percent to 65 percent of students with or without disabilities who engage in misconduct are given out-of-school suspension. The length of suspension is about the same and less than half of the suspended students with or without disabilities receive educational services during their suspensions. It seems that the argument that IDEA promotes violence is unfounded; in fact, principals interviewed during the GAO study indicated that IDEA plays a limited role in affecting schools' ability to properly discipline students.

Children with Disabilities and School Violence

Students with disabilities who are considered at potential risk for committing violent acts in school include children with learning disabilities, emotional disabilities, and attention deficit hyperactivity disorder (ADHD). . . .

According to S. Burrel and L. Warboys, "disabilities that are frequently encountered among delinquents include emotional disturbance, specific learning disabilities, mental retardation, other health impairments (such as ADHD), and speech or language impairment." The two most common disabilities found in the juvenile justice system are specific learning disabilities and emotional disturbance.

SRI International conducted a National Longitudinal Transition Study from 1987 to 1993 and found that arrest rates increased over time among youth with disabilities, from 19 percent when they had been out of secondary school up to two years to 30 percent three years later. Furthermore, arrest rates were highest and increased most dramatically for youth with serious emotional disturbances. Two years out of high school, 37 percent had been arrested. By the time youth with disabilities had been out of school three to five years, 58 percent had been arrested at some time. Arrest rates also were relatively high for youth with learning disabilities (31 percent had been arrested three to five years after high school). Arrest rates were less than 20 percent for most other disability categories and less than 10 percent for youth with orthopedic and other health impairments and youth who were deaf/blind. The arrest rate three to five years after secondary school was 56 percent among high school dropouts, compared with 16 percent among graduates and 10 percent among those who aged out of school. Among dropouts with serious emotional disturbances, the arrest rate was 73 percent.

Emotional Disturbance and Juvenile Delinquency

The relationship between emotional or behavioral disorders and serious juvenile problems is strong. The potential for serious juvenile problems is clear in young boys and girls.

- Problem behaviors are clearly established by ages 4 to 5.
- Overt (e.g., bullying) and covert (e.g., stealing) antisocial activities are becoming behavior patterns.
- Problems happen across settings (home, school, community).
- The child is both overactive and inattentive.
- Extreme aggression is frequent.

Of these five characteristics of young children prone to later problems, the single best predictor is aggression. For example, 6th graders referred to special education because of both violent and nonviolent inappropriate behaviors are likely to present chronic discipline problems during their remaining school years. The strong relationship between emotional disturbance and juvenile delinquency has served as a catalyst for some researchers to question the common factors of the school shootings and characteristics of students with emotional disturbance. T.H. Shubert, S. Bressette, J. Deeker, and W.N. Bender examined the school-yard shootings that occurred from October 1997 to May 1998 in Pearl, Mississippi; West Paducah, Kentucky; Jonesborough, Arkansas; Edinboro, Pennsylvania; and Springfield, Oregon, to determine common factors among the violent young perpetrators. One common factor noted was that although no one was identified as having a disability, "each demonstrated some indicators to peers of fairly serious emotional problems."

After subsequent school-yard shootings in Littleton, Colorado, and Conyers, Georgia, Bender, [Shubert, and P.J. McLaughlin] analyzed the shootings to determine common factors of the violent perpetrators. When comparing Shubert et al.'s analysis with Bender et al.'s analysis, similar findings were noted. For example, Bender et al. noted that "each of the students responsible for the shootings demonstrated some type of emotional trouble."

Learning Disabilities and Delinquency

The link between learning disabilities and delinquency is not clear. Early research studies suggested that students with learning disabilities (LD) were at greater risk for delinquency than their nondisabled peers. In fact, three hypotheses were posed as the causal explanations for the link between LD and delinquency. The first hypothesis, school failure, suggests that students with LD experience academic failure, which leads to the development of a negative self-image, which in turn leads to school dropout and delinquency. A second hypothesis is the differential treatment hypothesis, which postulates that students with LD engage in delinquent acts at the same rates as nondisabled peers but are more likely to be arrested or adjudicated. The third hypothesis, the susceptibility hypothesis, proposes that children with LD frequently have "a variety of troublesome personality characteristics," [as C.A. Murray writes].

Despite reports that students with learning disabilities are frequently among juvenile delinquents, and a number of professionals have speculated that learning disabilities contribute to the increased risk for delinquent behavior, empirical data supporting a causal relationship does not exist. In fact, recent research suggests that there is no relationship between LD and delinquency. K. Malmgren, R.D. Abbott, and J.D. Hawkins examined longitudinal data from a seven-year prospective study to determine whether the presence of LD increased a youth's risk for becoming a juvenile delinquent. The results did not confirm a direct relationship between LD and delinquency.

The authors also suggest that findings of positive correlation noted in earlier studies may have been due to confounding variables such as LD and age, LD and ethnicity, and LD and socioeconomic status.

Neurological Impairment

Although recent research findings suggest that there is no correlation between LD and delinquency, some researchers have examined the relationship between neurological impairment and violence. Neuroimaging research studies such as positron emission tomography (PET), single photon emission computed tomography (SPECT), and functional magnetic resonance imaging (fMRI) have been conducted to examine violence and aggression. For example, N.D. Volkow et al. and A. Raine et al. used PET scans to determine that decreased glucose metabolism in the prefrontal and medial temporal cortex was associated with increased aggressive behaviors in adults.

D. Amen conducted brain studies using SPECT and found that adolescents and adults with aggressiveness showed abnormalities of cerebral blood flow in the frontal and temporal lobes. Using fMRI, K. Rubia et al. found abnormal frontal lobe function in adolescents; similar findings were noted in G. Bush et al.'s study of adults with attention deficit disorder. Most recently, V. Matthews found that when children diagnosed with oppositional defiant disorder or conduct disorder were exposed to media violence, they demonstrated less activation in the frontal lobe. M.C. Brower and B.H. Price examined the link between frontal lobe dysfunction and violent and criminal behavior. They concluded that clinically significant frontal lobe dysfunction is associated with aggressive behavior, with impulsivity having the strongest relationship. Furthermore, they found that no study had reliably demonstrated a characteristic pattern of frontal network dysfunction predictive of violent crime. However, R.B. Flannery and D. Weinberger postulate that brain development can contribute to school violence. Weinberger believes that "school shootings occur because the prefrontal cortex in a teenage brain is not fully developed." The prefrontal cortex is part of the brain that enables people to act rationally and resist violent impulses. However, the cortex is not fully functional until adulthood. Consequently, it is believed that adolescents responsible for school shootings are unable to control their impulses and are unaware of the long-range consequences of their actions. Neurodevelopment research has also focused on the possibility that abuse and neglect, particularly during infancy and early childhood, may negatively affect brain development because of either physical injury or neurochemical alterations in response to trauma. Altered neural structures may prevent children from developing impulse control skills.

Other students who are considered at risk for committing delinquent and violent acts are children with attention deficit hyperactivity disorder (ADHD). In fact, the 2001 U.S. Surgeon General's report identified ADHD as a risk factor for violence in youths aged 6–11. According to Burrell and Warboys and J.H. Williams and R.A. Van Dorn, four characteristics of ADHD—hyperactivity, concentration problems, restlessness, and risk-taking behaviors—have been found to be strong predictors of violent behavior. These characteristics, as well as poor social skills and certain beliefs and attitudes, such as seeing the need for retaliation, appear to favor the development of delinquent behavior. In addition, students with ADHD are more likely to display antisocial behavior, which is considered a risk factor for aggression later in adulthood and violent actions. R. Loeber points out that ADHD is also associated with early onset of delinquency and is correlated with persistent disruptive behavior.

Researchers have examined one or more of the ADHD characteristics and its relationship to violence or delinquent behavior. For example, concentration problems of boys ages 8 to 14 were significant predictors of self-reported violence and official arrests for violent offenses for males between the ages of 10 and 32 in a British study. B. Klinteberg, [T. Andersson, D. Magnusson, and H. Stattin] examined restlessness (for example, difficulty sitting still, talkativeness) as measured by teacher reports and determined that restlessness is associated with later violence in adulthood. Several researchers have found that childhood hyperactivity is related to violence in adulthood. Others have found that restlessness, poor concentration, impulsivity, and risk taking in childhood predict later violence. J.D. Hawkins et al. conducted a meta-analysis and found small positive correlations between childhood/adolescent hyperactivity, concentration problems, restlessness, and impulsivity.

One form of treatment for ADHD is Ritalin. K.P. O'Meara points out that many of the adolescent perpetrators in the high profiled schoolyard shootings that occurred between 1996 and 1999 were taking psychotropic drugs, Ritalin, Prozac, and Luvox. She states that these drugs have been known to cause psychotic episodes and violent behavior in some patients and may have played a part in the violent acts. In addition, she believes that although side effects have been recorded, the drugs continue to be prescribed at alarmingly high rates. "There are nearly 6 million children in the United States between the ages 6 and 18 taking mind-altering drugs prescribed for alleged illnesses that increasing numbers of mental health professionals are questioning." However, no research suggests there is a correlation between the recent cases of violent behavior in school-age children and the widespread use of psychotropic drugs such as Ritalin, Prozac, or Luvox.

The Role of Special Education

Some schools have responded to school violence by placing children in special education, while others are looking at the possibility of children who have disabilities are at risk for committing violent acts. Although special education services are provided to students with special needs and these services help address individual student's needs such as aggressive behavior, special education should not be considered the solution for violence prevention, especially if the child is not eligible for special education services. Based on the 2002 Secret Service report we know that none of the targeted school shootings were committed by children with special needs.

ADOLESCENT MASCULINITY, HOMOPHOBIA, AND VIOLENCE

Michael S. Kimmel and Matthew Mahler

In the following selection, Michael S. Kimmel and Matthew Mahler point out that few studies about the causes of school violence have addressed what may be the most important factor: the gender of the assailants. The overwhelming majority of school shootings have been perpetrated by white males, Kimmel and Mahler note. Furthermore, they maintain, most of these shootings have taken place at suburban or rural schools in relatively conservative areas of the nation, where there is little tolerance for shy or studious boys who do not fit stereotypical conventions of masculinity. The common denominator in recent school shootings, the authors argue, is that all of the shooters were bullied and teased with homophobic remarks. Kimmel and Mahler contend that the assailants resorted to violence in a desperate attempt to recover a sense of masculine power. Kimmel is a professor of sociology and Mahler is a graduate student, both at the State University of New York at Stony Brook.

> Generally speaking, violence always arises out of impotence.
> It is the hope of those who have no power.
> —Hannah Arendt

Violence is one of the most urgent issues facing our nation's schools. All over the country, Americans are asking why some young people open fire, apparently randomly, killing or wounding other students and their teachers. Are these teenagers emotionally disturbed? Are they held in the thrall of media-generated violence—in video games, the Internet, rock or rap music? Are their parents to blame?

The Seriousness of the Problem

Indeed, school violence is an issue that weighs heavily on our nation's consciousness. Students report being increasingly afraid to go to school; among young people aged 12 to 24, 3 in 10 say violence has

Michael S. Kimmel and Matthew Mahler, "Adolescent Masculinity, Homophobia, and Violence," *American Behavioral Scientist*, vol. 46, June 2003, pp. 1,439–1,449. Copyright © 2003 by Sage Publications, Inc. Reproduced by permission.

increased in their schools in the past year and nearly two-fifths have worried that a classmate was potentially violent. More than half of all teens know somebody who has brought a weapon to school (although more than three-fifths of them did nothing about it), according to a PAX[1] study. And nearly two-thirds (63%) of parents believe a school shooting is somewhat or very likely to occur in their communities. The shock, concern, and wrenching anguish shared by both children and parents who fear that our nation's schools may not be safe demands serious policy discussions. And such discussions demand serious inquiry into the causes of school violence.

We begin our inquiry with an analysis of the extant commentary and literature on school violence. We argue that, unfortunately, there are significant lacunae in all of these accounts—the most significant of which is the fact that they all ignore the one factor that cuts across all cases of random school shootings—masculinity. Thus, we argue that any approach to understanding school shootings must take gender seriously—specifically the constellation of adolescent masculinity, homophobia, and violence.

We go on to argue that in addition to taking gender seriously, a reasoned approach to understanding school shootings must focus not on the *form* of the shootings—not on questions of family history, psychological pathologies, or broad-based cultural explanations (violence in the media, proliferation of guns) but on the *content* of the shootings—the stories and narratives that accompany the violence, the relationships and interactions among students, and local school and gender cultures. Using such an approach to interpret the various events that led up to each of the shootings, we find that a striking similarity emerges between the various cases. All or most of the shooters had tales of being harassed—specifically, gay-baited—for inadequate gender performance; their tales are the tales of boys who did not measure up to the norms of hegemonic masculinity. Thus, in our view, these boys are not psychopathological deviants but rather overconformists to a particular normative construction of masculinity, a construction that defines violence as a legitimate response to a perceived humiliation.

Missing the Mark

The concern over school shootings has prompted intense national debate, in recent years, over who or what is to blame. One need not look hard to find any number of "experts" who are willing to weigh in on the issue. Yet despite the legion of political and scientific commentaries on school shootings, these voices have all singularly and spectacularly missed the point.

1. PAX is a nonpartisan organization that seeks to end gun violence in the United States.

At the vanguard of the debates have been politicians. Some have argued that Goth music, Marilyn Manson, and violent video games are the causes of school shootings. Then-president Bill Clinton argued that it might be the Internet; Newt Gingrich credited the 1960s; and Tom DeLay blamed daycare, the teaching of evolution, and "working mothers who take birth control pills." Political pundits and media commentators also have offered a host of possible explanations, of which one of the more popular answers has been violence in the media. "Parents don't realize that taking four year-olds to *True Lies*—a fun movie for adults but excessively violent—is poison to their brain," notes Michael Gurian. Alvin Poussaint, a psychiatrist at Harvard Medical School, wrote that

> in America, violence is considered fun to kids. They play video games where they chop people's heads off and blood gushes and it's fun, it's entertainment. It's like a game. And I think this is the psychology of these kids—this "Let's go out there and kill like on television."

And Sissela Bok, in her erudite warning on violence, *Mayhem*, suggests that the Internet and violent video games, which "bring into homes depictions of graphic violence . . . never available to children and young people in the past," undermine kids' resilience and self-control.

For others, the staggering statistics linking youth violence and the availability of guns point to a possible cause. Firearms are the second leading cause of death to children between age 10 and 14 and the eighth leading cause of death to those age 1 to 4. In 1994, 80% of juvenile murders used a firearm; in 1984, only 50% did. Barry Krisberg, president of the National Council on Crime and Delinquency, argues that both the media and guns are at fault. He says, "The violence in the media and the easy availability of guns are what is driving the slaughter of innocents." Or perhaps, if we are to believe National Rifle Association (NRA) president Charlton Heston, the problem is not that there are too many guns but that there are not enough guns. He argues that had there been armed guards in the schools, the shooting would have ended instantly. These accounts, however, that blame a media purportedly overly saturated by violence and a society infatuated with guns are undercut by two important facts, which are often conveniently forgotten amid the fracas. The first is that whereas the amount of violent media content has ostensibly been increasing, both youth violence, in general, and school violence, in particular, have actually been decreasing since 1980. And second, juvenile violence involving guns has been in decline since 1994 (largely as a result of the decline of the crack epidemic). As Michael Carneal, the boy who shot his classmates in Paducah, Kentucky, said, "I don't know why it happened, but I know it wasn't a movie."

Finally, some have proposed psychological variables, including a history of childhood abuse, absent fathers, dominant mothers, violence in childhood, unstable family environment, or the mothers' fear of their children, as possible explanations. Although these explanations are all theoretically possible, empirically, it appears as though none of them holds up. Almost all the shooters came from intact and relatively stable families, with no history of child abuse. If they had psychological problems at all, they were relatively minor, and the boys flew under the radar of any school official or family member who might have noticed something seriously wrong. In a term paper, Eric Harris, of Columbine infamy, quoted Shakespeare's *The Tempest*, "Good wombs hath borne bad sons."

The Missing Link: Gender

This search for causal variables is also misguided because it ignores a crucial component of all the shootings. These childhood variables would apply equally to boys and to girls. Thus, they offer little purchase with which to answer the question of why it is that only boys open fire on their classmates.

Government-supported investigations, such as the Federal Bureau of Investigation's (FBI) report, the Surgeon General's report on youth violence . . . , the Bureau of Justice Statistics' *Indicators of School Crime and Safety, 2000*, as well as the latest study of bullying all concentrate on identifying potential psychological or cultural antecedents of school violence, for example, media influence, drugs and alcohol behavior, Internet usage, father absence, and parental neglect. That is to say, they focus on "form"—who the perpetrators were—not the "content." None examine local cultures, local school cultures, or gender as an antecedent or risk factor.

Most important for our argument is the fact that these studies have all missed gender. They use such broad terminology as "teen violence," "youth violence," "gang violence," "suburban violence," and "violence in the schools" as though girls are equal participants in this violence. Conspicuously absent is any mention of just who these youth or teens are who have committed the violence. They pay little or no attention to the obvious fact that *all the school shootings were committed by boys*—masculinity is the single greatest risk factor in school violence. This uniformity cuts across all other differences among the shooters: Some came from intact families, others from single-parent homes; some boys had acted violently in the past, others were quiet and unsuspecting; and some boys also expressed rage at their parents (two killed their parents the same morning), whereas others seemed to live in happy families. And yet, if the killers in the schools in Littleton, Pearl, Paducah, Springfield, and Jonesboro had all been girls, gender would undoubtedly be the only story. Someone might even blame feminism for causing girls to become violent in vain imitation of boys.

But the analytic blindness of these studies runs deeper than gender. We can identify two different waves of school violence since 1980. In the first, from 1982 to 1991, the majority of all the school shootings were nonrandom (i.e., the victims were specifically targeted by the perpetrators). Most were in urban, inner-city schools and involved students of color. Virtually all involved handguns, all were sparked by disputes over girlfriends or drugs, and all were committed by boys.

These cases have not entirely disappeared, but they have declined dramatically. Since 1992, only 1 of the random school shootings occurred in inner-city schools (it was committed by a Black student), whereas the remaining 22 have been committed by White students in suburban schools. Virtually all involved rifles, not handguns—a symbolic shift from urban to rural weaponry. However, once again, all shootings were committed by boys.

As the race and class of the perpetrators have shifted, so too has the public perception of school violence. No longer do we hear claims about the "inherent" violence of the inner city or, what is even more pernicious, the "inherently" violent tendencies of certain racial or ethnic groups. As the shooters have become White and suburban middle-class boys, the public has shifted the blame away from group characteristics to individual psychological problems, assuming that these boys were deviants who broke away from an otherwise genteel suburban culture—that their aberrant behavior was explainable by some psychopathological factor. Although it is no doubt true that many of the boys who committed these terrible acts did have serious psychological problems, such a framing masks the significant role that race and class, in addition to gender, play in school violence. If all the school shooters had been poor African American boys in inner-city schools, it is much less likely that their acts would have been seen as deviant or pathological. Instead, discussions would have centered on the effects of the culture of poverty or the "normality" of violence among inner-city youth.

Who Shoots and Why?

Still, most students—White or non-White, male or female—are not violent, schools are predominantly safe, and school shootings are aberrations. As a public, we seem concerned with school shootings because its story is not "when children kill" but specifically when suburban White boys kill. . . .

[The data] reveal that school shootings do not occur uniformly or evenly in the United States, which makes one skeptical of uniform cultural explanations such as violent video games, musical tastes, Internet, television, and movies. School shootings are decidedly *not* a national trend. Of 28 school shootings between 1982 and 2001, all but 1 were in rural or suburban schools (1 in Chicago). All but 2 (Chicago again and Virginia Beach) were committed by a White boy or boys.

The Los Angeles school district has had no school shootings since 1984; in 1999, San Francisco, which has several programs to identify potentially violent students, had only two kids bring guns to school.

School shootings can be divided even further, along the lines of a deep and familiar division in American society.

Contrary to Alan Wolfe's assertion that we are "one nation, after all," it appears that we are actually two nations: "red states" (states that voted for George W. Bush in the 2000 presidential election) and "blue states" (states that voted for Al Gore in the 2000 election). Of the 28 school shootings, 20 took place in red states. Of those in the blue states, 1 was in suburban Oregon, 1 was in rural (Eastern) Washington, 2 were in Southern California, 1 was in rural and another in suburban Pennsylvania, 1 was in rural New Mexico, and 1 was in Chicago. Of those 8 from blue states, half of the counties in those blue states (Santee, CA; Red Hill, PA; Moses Lake, WA; and Deming, NM) voted Republican in the last election.

From Form to Content

What this suggests is that school violence is unevenly distributed and that to understand its causes, we must look locally—both at "gun culture" (percentage of homes owning firearms, gun registrations, NRA memberships), local gender culture, and local school cultures—attitudes about gender nonconformity, tolerance of bullying, and teacher attitudes. We need to focus less on the form of school violence—documenting its prevalence and presenting a demographic profile of the shooters—and more on the *content* of the shootings; instead of asking psychological questions about family dynamics and composition, psychological problems, and pathologies, we need to focus our attention on local school cultures and hierarchies, peer interactions, normative gender ideologies, and the interactions among academics, adolescence, and gender identity.

With this as our guiding theoretical framework, we undertook an analysis of secondary media reports on *random school shootings from 1982 to 2001*. Using the shooters' names as our search terms, we gathered articles from six major media sources—the three major weekly news magazines: *Time, Newsweek,* and *U.S. News and World Report* (in order from greatest circulation to least); and three major daily newspapers: *USA Today, The New York Times,* and the *Los Angeles Times*. In conducting our analysis, we found a striking pattern from the stories about the boys who committed the violence: Nearly all had stories of being constantly bullied, beat up, and, most significantly for this analysis, "gay-baited." Nearly all had stories of being mercilessly and constantly teased, picked on, and threatened. And most strikingly, it was *not* because they were gay (at least there is no evidence to suggest that any of them were gay) but because they were *different* from the other boys—shy, bookish, honor students, artistic, musical, theatrical, nonathletic, "geekish," or weird. Theirs are stories of "cultural marginalization" based on criteria for adequate gender performance, specifically the enactment of codes of masculinity.

In a recent interview, the eminent gender theorist Eminem poignantly illustrated the role of "gay-baiting" in peer interactions. In his view, calling someone a "faggot" is not a slur on his sexuality but on his gender. He says,

> The lowest degrading thing that you can say to a man . . . is to call him a faggot and try to take away his manhood. Call him a sissy. Call him a punk. "Faggot" to me doesn't necessarily mean gay people. "Faggot" to me just means taking away your manhood.

In this rationalization, Eminem, perhaps unwittingly, speaks to the central connection between gender and sexuality and particularly to the association of gender nonconformity with homosexuality. Here, homophobia is far less about the irrational fears of gay people, or the fears that one might actually be gay or have gay tendencies, and more the fears that *heterosexuals* have that others might *(mis)perceive them as gay*. Research has indicated that homophobia is one of the organizing principles of heterosexual masculinity, a constitutive element in its construction. And as an organizing principle of masculinity, homophobia—the terror that others will see one as gay, as a failed man—underlies a significant amount of men's behavior, including their relationships with other men, women, and violence. One could say that homophobia is the hate that makes men straight.

There is much at stake for boys and, as a result, they engage in a variety of evasive strategies to make sure that no one gets the wrong idea about them (and their manhood). These range from the seemingly comic (although telling), such as two young boys occupying three movie seats by placing their coats on the seat between them, to the truly tragic, such as engaging in homophobic violence, bullying, menacing other boys, masochistic or sadistic games and rituals, excessive risk taking (drunk or aggressive driving), and even sexual predation and assault. The impact of homophobia is felt not only by gay and lesbian students but also by heterosexuals who are targeted by their peers for constant harassment, bullying, and gay-baiting. In many cases, gay-baiting is "misdirected" at heterosexual youth who may be somewhat gender nonconforming. This fact is clearly evidenced in many of the accounts we have gathered of the shootings.

Accounts of Homophobic Bullying

For example, young Andy Williams, recently sentenced to 50 years to life in prison for shooting and killing two classmates in Santee, California, and wounding several others was described as "shy" and was "constantly picked on" by others in school. Like many of the others, bullies stole his clothes, his money, and his food, beat him up regularly, and locked him in his locker, among other daily taunts and humiliations. One boy's father baited him and called him a "queer" because he was overweight. Classmates described Gary Scott Pennington, who killed his teacher and a custodian in Grayson, Kentucky, in 1993 as a "nerd" and a "loner" who was constantly teased for being smart and wearing glasses. Barry Loukaitis, who killed his algebra teacher and two other students in Moses Lake, Washington, in 1996 was an honor student who especially loved math; he was also constantly teased and bullied and described as a "shy nerd." And Evan Ramsey, who killed one student and the high school principal in Bethel, Alaska, in 1997 was also an honor student who was teased for wearing glasses and having acne.

Luke Woodham was a bookish and overweight 16-year-old in Pearl, Mississippi. An honor student, he was part of a little group that studied Latin and read Nietzsche. Students teased him constantly for being overweight and a nerd and taunted him as "gay" or "fag." Even his mother called him fat, stupid, and lazy. Other boys bullied him routinely and, according to one fellow student, he "never fought back when other boys called him names." On October 1, 1997, Woodham stabbed his mother to death in her bed before he left for school. He then drove her car to school, carrying a rifle under his coat. He opened fire in the school's common area, killing two students and wounding seven others. After being subdued, he told the assistant principal, "The world has wronged me." Later, in a psychiatric interview, he said,

> I am not insane. I am angry. . . . I am not spoiled or lazy; for murder is not weak and slow-witted; murder is gutsy and daring. I killed because people like me are mistreated every day. I am malicious because I am miserable.

Fourteen-year-old Michael Carneal was a shy and frail freshman at Heath High School in Paducah, Kentucky, barely 5 feet tall, weighing 110 pounds. He wore thick glasses and played in the high school band. He felt alienated, pushed around, and picked on. Boys stole his lunch and constantly teased him. In middle school, someone pulled down his pants in front of his classmates. He was so hypersensitive and afraid that others would see him naked that he covered the air vents in the bathroom. He was devastated when students called him a "faggot" and almost cried when the school gossip sheet labeled him "gay." On Thanksgiving, 1997, he stole two shotguns, two semiautomatic rifles, a pistol, and 700 rounds of ammunition and after a weekend of showing them off to his classmates, brought them to school hoping that they would bring him some instant recognition. "I just wanted the guys to think I was cool" he said. When the cool guys ignored him, he opened fire on a morning prayer circle, killing three classmates and wounding five others. Now serving a life sentence in prison, Carneal told psychiatrists weighing his sanity, "People respect me now."

Homophobia at Columbine High School

At Columbine High School, the site of the nation's most infamous school shooting, this connection was not lost on Evan Todd, a 255-pound defensive lineman on the Columbine football team, an exemplar of the jock culture that Dylan Klebold and Eric Harris found to be such an interminable torment. "Columbine is a clean, good place, except for those rejects," Todd said.

> Sure we teased them. But what do you expect with kids who come to school with weird hairdos and horns on their hats? It's not just jocks; the whole school's disgusted with them. They're a bunch of homos. . . . If you want to get rid of someone, usually you tease 'em. So the whole school would call them homos.

Ben Oakley, a soccer player, agreed. "Nobody liked them," he said, "The majority of them were gay. So everyone would make fun of them." Athletes taunted them: "Nice dress" they'd say. They would throw rocks and bottles at them from moving cars. The school newspaper had recently published a rumor that Harris and Klebold were lovers.

Both were reasonably well-adjusted kids. Harris's parents were a retired Army officer and a caterer—decent, well-intentioned people. Klebold's father was a geophysicist who had recently moved into the mortgage services business and his mother worked in job placement for the disabled. Harris had been rejected by several colleges; Klebold was due to enroll at Arizona in the fall. But the jock culture was relentless. Said one friend,

> Every time someone slammed them against a locker and threw a bottle at them, I think they'd go back to Eric or Dylan's house and plot a little more—at first as a goof, but more and more seriously over time.

The rest is all too familiar. Harris and Klebold brought a variety of weapons to their high school and proceeded to walk through the school, shooting whomever they could find. Students were terrified and tried to hide. Many students who could not hide begged for their lives. The entire school was held under siege until the police secured the building. In all, 23 students and faculty were injured and 15 died, including one teacher and the perpetrators.

In the videotape made the night before the shootings, Harris says, "People constantly make fun of my face, my hair, my shirts." Klebold adds, "I'm going to kill you all. You've been giving us shit for years." What Klebold said he had been receiving for years apparently included constant gay-baiting, being called "queer," "faggot," "homo," being pushed into lockers, grabbed in hallways, and mimicked and ridiculed with homophobic slurs. For some boys, high school is a constant homophobic gauntlet and they may respond by becoming withdrawn and sullen, using drugs or alcohol, becoming depressed or suicidal, or acting out in a blaze of overcompensating violent "glory."

The Effects of Homophobic Hectoring

The prevalence of this homophobic bullying, teasing, and violence is staggering. According to the Gay, Lesbian, Straight Education Network, 97% of students in public high school in Massachusetts reported regularly hearing homophobic remarks from their peers in 1993; 53% reported hearing anti-gay remarks by school staff. The [2001] report *Hatred in the Hallways* paints a bleak picture of anti-gay harassment but pays significant attention to the ways in which gender performance—acting masculine—is perceived as a code for heterosexuality.

And if we are to believe recent research, the effects of such hectoring should not be underestimated. In a national survey of teenagers' attitudes, students suggested that peer harassment was the most significant cause of school shootings. Nearly 9 of 10 teenagers said that they believed that the school shootings were motivated by a desire "to get back at those who have hurt them" (87%) and that "other kids picking on them, making fun of them, or bullying them" (86%) were the immediate causes. Other potential causes such as violence on television, movies, computer games, or videos (37%); boredom (18%); mental problems (56%); access to guns (56%); and prior physical victimization at home (61%) were significantly lower on the adolescents' ratings. "If it's anyone it'll be the kids that are ostracized, picked on, and constantly made fun of," commented one boy.

Also interesting is the fact that in all four geographic regions of the country—East, South, Midwest, and West—students in rural high schools rated their schools as most dangerous; in the South and West, students in suburban high schools thought their schools more dangerous than urban schools. Equally interesting is that perceptions of issues related to school shooting varied by race, because Blacks are less likely than other racial groups to believe that getting back at others could be a reason for violence, less likely to see bullying as a significant problem than Whites, and less likely to believe that lack of friends could be blamed for school violence. . . .

Let us be completely clear: Our hypotheses are decidedly *not* that gay and lesbian youth are more likely to open fire on their fellow students. In fact, from all available evidence, *none* of the school shooters was gay. But that is our organizing hypothesis: Homophobia—being constantly threatened and bullied *as if you are gay* as well as the homophobic desire to make sure that others know that you are a "real man"—plays a pivotal and understudied role in these school shootings. But more than just taking gender performance and its connections to homosexuality seriously, we argue that we must also carefully investigate the dynamics of gender within these local cultures, especially local school cultures and the typically hegemonic position of jock culture and its influence on normative assumptions of masculinity, to begin to understand what pushes some boys toward such horrific events, what sorts of pressures keep most boys cowed in silence, and what resources enable some boys to resist.

CHAPTER 3

SCHOOL VIOLENCE: PERSONAL NARRATIVES

Contemporary Issues
Companion

Paying the Price: School Shooters Speak Out from Prison

Timothy Roche and Amanda Bower

Timothy Roche and Amanda Bower are reporters for *Time* magazine. In this selection written in 2001, Roche and Bower profile twelve school shooters who are serving time in prison for their crimes. Most of these young convicts are starting to understand the impact of their actions, the authors reveal, and are experiencing intense feelings of remorse. They suffer from nightmares, flashbacks, depression, and suicidal impulses, Roche and Bower explain. In addition, some of these boys have become increasingly isolated as friends, family members, and even their parents cut off contact with them. According to the authors, the school shooters not only have to cope with the typical hardships of prison life but also the realization that they have destroyed their own futures for a fleeting moment of revenge or glory.

"Not too bad," that's what the boy killer murmured to his lawyer when the verdict came in. He was right that it could have been worse. The Florida jury might have gone for murder one but instead convicted Nathaniel Brazill, 14, of murder in the second degree for pointing a gun between the eyes of his favorite teacher and pulling the trigger a year ago. "I'm O.K.," he mouthed to his mother Polly, seated in the courtroom's second row. Then he gave a little wave to a young cousin, sitting nearby.

If Brazill didn't at that instant grasp the grim future that awaits him, it probably won't take him long. Next month the judge will mete out a sentence that could mean a lifetime in prison. And if Brazill needs a clearer picture of what's in store for him, the prison life of other school shooters will give him an idea. These young gunmen, at the moment of their wrathful outbursts, were often filled with a sense of potency and triumph or at least relief that whatever or whoever was troubling them had been exorcised. But those sensations generally prove fleeting. As they settle into the monotony and isolation of prison life, these boys tend to experience feelings of profound regret, remorse and loss as they come to terms with what they have done to their victims and what they have done to themselves.

For eight weeks, TIME delved into the lives of 12 convicted school shooters—who had terrified their classmates and periodically traumatized the nation since 1997. Among them, they fired 135 shots, killing 21 people and wounding 62. If they were not suffering overtly from mental illness before their crimes, many clearly are now, with varying degrees of treatment available. Psychologists say they are likely to be suicidal for much of their lives and suffer repeated flashbacks to the single day when everything changed, when they killed beloved teachers or gunned down schoolmates they did not know, when they went from good sons to the young terrorists among us.

Within the system and in their own personal circles, these boys engender a wide range of reactions. Prosecutors label many of them unredeemable sociopaths; defenders say that with education and counseling, they can be restored. Even loved ones take varying positions. Some offer support, while others abandon their own.

To this day, a few of the boys refuse to explain themselves. And it is fair to ask why we would want to hear from any of them anyway or have sympathy for what they have to say. But many have developed, sometimes with the help of psychologists, a better understanding of what led them to murderous fury—an understanding that could help others avoid such atrocities in the future. Almost all the shooters were expressing rage, either against a particular person for a particular affront or, more often, against a whole cohort of bullying classmates. Some of their stories confirm the notion that school shootings are a contagion, that the perpetrators are imitating the gross acts of carnage they've seen reported in other places. On the day that he brought to school a .25-cal. semiautomatic handgun that he had stolen from his grandfather's desk drawer, Brazill boasted to a classmate that he would be "all over the news."

If these kids felt empowered by the notorious shooters who came before them, however, at least some—the most self-aware of the group—now want to set a new example for students tempted to perpetuate the cycle. Don't look to Columbine's Dylan Klebold and Eric Harris, the most notorious of the school avengers, this group is saying. Those boys killed themselves and never had to face the aftermath of their rampage. Instead, this group says, look to us, who are living the postscript, and don't let it happen to you. Even Brazill, in an interview with TIME six weeks before his conviction, had come that far. Asked what he would like to tell the student groups who sometimes tour his jail, he replied, "Don't pick up a gun. You don't know what's going to happen."

The Price

Evan Ramsey knows. Four years ago, he brought a pump-action shotgun to his Alaska high school and opened up, killing the principal and one student. Now he is serving a 210-year term in a maximum-security prison in the Alaskan mountains. Every night, before crashing in the tiny cell he shares with a fellow murderer, he mops the prison floors, a job that earns him $21 a month, just enough to buy soap, shampoo and stationery, which the Spring Creek Correctional Center does not supply for free. His face pasty white from lack of sun, Ramsey told TIME his biggest complaint is the total absence of privacy. The light is always on in his cell, and the toilet sits in the open at the end of his bunk.

A school shooter with one of the longest sentences, Ramsey has encountered some of the harder edges of prison life. He spent six months in solitary confinement after beating a fellow inmate with a sock packed with batteries when the prisoner reneged on a gambling debt of four candy bars. Ramsey has heard that an uncle of the student he killed is in the same prison and that the man "wants to do a bunch of different things to me."

Ramsey says he committed his rampage because he was sick of being picked on in school, where he was nicknamed "Screech," after the geeky character in the TV show *Saved by the Bell.* "Nobody liked me, and I could never understand why," he says. "It was pretty bad then, but it's a lot worse now." Sometimes Ramsey will be starkly reminded of the shooting, for instance, when he recently received papers on a civil suit his victims' families have filed against the school district. "I sit there, and I wish, I wish, I wish, I wish I didn't do what I did," he says. "I wish I would have known the things that I know now."

Among Ramsey's wishes is that one of the two friends to whom he confided his lethal plan would have turned him in. Last week a blue-ribbon panel that studied the Columbine massacre criticized police, school officials and the killers' parents for not intervening to stop Klebold and Harris, after being given signs of their murderous intent. "That would have been one of the best things a person could have done," says Ramsey of his own case. Instead, Ramsey's buddies egged him on.

Maintaining relationships from within prison walls is a trial. Some of these kids have devoted parents and friends. A number have attracted admirers. Ramsey has a pen-pal fiancee. Kip Kinkel, who is serving a 112-year term for killing his parents and then two students in his Oregon high school in 1998, has received money in the mail from strangers. Charles (Andy) Williams, who is in prison on charges of killing two students in his Santee, Calif., school in March, gets more letters than he can answer—as many as 40 a week, according to his lawyer. There are five different clubs on Yahoo dedicated to him, as well as a dozen homemade websites. But the real, deepest ties these kids have to their communities are often shredded. Ramsey's family visits only once a year. At one point, they went nine months without even calling.

The father of Mitchell Johnson, who with buddy Andrew Golden killed four kids and a teacher when they attacked their Jonesboro, Ark., school with an arsenal of weapons in 1998, has severed contact with him. Mitchell told his mother that his father said to him on the phone, "You're the reason I quit praying" and hung up. After T.J. Solomon of Conyers, Ga., shot and wounded six classmates with a sawed-off shotgun in 1999, his mother demanded to know why he hadn't blasted himself. "You were going to kill yourself, I understand. How did that not happen?" she asked him just after his arrest. "I don't understand how you took innocent children, but you were too afraid to do anything to you. That really has me puzzled. You didn't think twice about doing it to them."

Luke Woodham, who killed two classmates in Pearl, Miss., in 1997 after beating and stabbing his mother to death, gets very few visitors. The school friends of Michael Carneal, who killed three classmates in West Paducah, Ky., in 1997, largely shun him. From jail, Brazill continued to write love letters to Dinora Rosales, one of the girls he wanted to see when the teacher he killed, Barry Grunow, refused to allow Brazill inside the classroom because he had been suspended for throwing water balloons. But the 14-year-old Rosales, feeling threatened, turned the mash notes over to the police.

The Remorse

After Jacob Davis used a magnum bolt-action rifle to mow down his girlfriend's ex-lover at his Tennessee high school in 1998, he dropped down beside the bleeding body. A friend came over and said to Davis, "Man, you just flushed your life down the toilet." Davis replied, "Yes, but it's been fun." The fun didn't last. Today Davis is serving a 52-year term at a medium-security correctional facility in Clifton, Tenn. Before the shooting, he had received an academic scholarship to study computer science at Mississippi State University. Instead, he takes a prison course to learn the low-tech skill of computer refurbishment. Dressed in prison blues, Davis spoke to TIME while seated at a small wooden table in a visitor's room, with a security guard standing watch in the corner.

"When you got someone else's blood on your hands, it's not an easy thing to deal with," Davis says, looking downward. "I will suffer my own personal hell the rest of my life. There's nothing you can do to make it go away. I'm truly remorseful for what happened. He's gone," Davis says of Nick Creson, the 18-year-old boy he killed, "and I can't do anything to change it and bring him back."

Davis is plagued by nightmares and insomnia, as are many of the other gunmen. And when he awakens each day, he often confronts anew the calamitous effects of his act on Creson's family and his own. "It's kind of hard not to when you wake up every morning in a prison cell," he says. If Johnson didn't understand at the time the consequences of his murders, he does now, says his mother Gretchen Woodard. "He's older. He knows now the permanence of it," she says. "If words from him would not hurt those families, he'd write them."

For many of the young shooters, news of another school rampage sets off bouts of emotional turmoil. Carneal became "seriously depressed" after the Columbine attack, according to Kentucky juvenile-justice commissioner Ralph Kelly. "He really took a setback from that. He felt a lot of responsibility for that happening." Kinkel also blamed himself for Columbine. On hearing the news, Kinkel told a psychologist, "I flipped out, started blaming myself." According to a friend, the March school shooting in Santee also disturbed Kinkel. Victor Cordova, incarcerated in a juvenile-treatment facility in New Mexico for shooting a schoolmate in the head, was so upset by a TV report on the Santee case that he asked to be released from the requirement that residents watch the evening news each day. Brazill, the night of his conviction, couldn't stomach even an episode of *Law & Order* that featured a school shooting; he retreated from the common room to his cell.

Woodham, whom many investigators believe started the chain of recent school shootings with his killing spree in 1997, is haunted by that burden. "If there's any way that I can, I would like to help stop these shootings," he wrote in a letter to TIME. Davis has the same idea and a plan. He's writing a book about his experiences. "I want somebody to learn from the mistakes I've gone through," he says. "I want to be a part of changing all this crap that's going on."

One way to do that is to try to understand the triggers for these crimes. Davis says for him the proximate cause was jealous rage. After his girlfriend, Tonya Bishop, confided that she had had sex with Creson, Davis became increasingly obsessed over a period of three months with hatred for Creson. Davis' stepmother Phyllis thought this was "just like any other" teen-romance drama and assumed that "just like everybody else, he'd get over it." He didn't. He was besotted with Bishop but didn't trust her. He started sleeping just a few hours a night. His grades fell from A's to D's and F's. One day, after a glaring match with Creson in a hallway, Davis recalls, "it was just like something clicked in my head. I had been going downhill for so long. I got stuck thinking about all the pain I'd suffered. And I couldn't put all that out of my head." He went home, got his hunting rifle and ambushed Creson in the school parking lot.

With the benefit of antidepressant medication, Davis now believes that mental illness was at the root of his behavior. The psychiatrists who examined him agree, having determined that at the time of the shooting, Davis was suffering from serious depression with psychotic features. Eight of the other 11 convicted kids that TIME reviewed have had some sort of mental disorder diagnosed since their crimes, mostly depression but also personality disorders and schizophrenia or its precursors. Six of the kids have had behavior-altering psychotropic drugs prescribed.

The presence of mental illness may help explain why some kids snap when faced with the usual torments of adolescence and others don't. Of course, some kids consider their vexations extraordinary. Carneal, who at the time of his crime was a freshman who got picked on for his small stature and quiet manner, told a psychiatrist that he felt going to prison would be better than continuing to endure the bullying in school.

Psychiatrist Stuart Twemlow, director of the Erik H. Erikson Institute for Education and Research in Stockbridge, Mass., notes that a significant subgroup of the school shooters consists of kids who come from relatively affluent families, who are academically above average, if not gifted, and who rarely have the qualities expected of violent offenders—such as a history of substance abuse or mental disorder. In Twemlow's view, this is no coincidence. "Bullying is more common in affluent schools probably than in the low-income schools," he says. It is spurred, he believes, by "the dynamics that come out of our typical hard-nosed, competitive" middle class.

Park Dietz, a forensic psychiatrist who has interviewed numerous school shooters, says they tend to have in common "some degree of depression, considerable anger, access to weapons that they aren't ready to have, and a role model salient in their memory. So far," he told a TIME reporter, "it's always been a mass murderer who has been given ample coverage in your magazine." Describing his pre-rampage mind-set, Solomon once wrote, "I felt the next thing left to release my anger would be through violence. I had just gotten the idea from the shooting at Columbine High School on April 20." Solomon opened fire precisely one month after that date. Seth Trickey, who in 1999 shot and wounded five classmates in Fort Gibson, Okla., told a psychiatrist he had become preoccupied with previous school shooters and wondered how he would hold up in their shoes. Woodham told the cops who took his confession, "I guess everyone is going to remember me now."

The Rehabilitation

Though Woodham has since expressed remorse, prison authorities aren't especially interested in his redemption. Woodham receives no schooling or counseling. "We don't make any pretense about trying to rehabilitate someone who is going to spend their natural life in prison," says Robert Johnson, commissioner of Mississippi's Department of Corrections. "What's the use?"

Most of the rest of the boys are working toward high school diplomas. A couple hope to move on to college correspondence courses. Seven of the shooters are offered regular psychological counseling, ranging from daily to weekly sessions. However, some lawyers and relatives have begun to question the treatment and challenge the qualifications of prison psychologists, who increasingly are overburdened and underfunded as overall inmate populations grow.

In Pennsylvania, the mother of Andrew Wurst, who opened fire on his middle-school dance in 1998, killing a teacher, has battled prison officials to upgrade her son's therapy. She has been rebuffed. So Wurst remains totally delusional, according to psychiatrist Robert Sadoff, who examined him. Sadoff wrote that Wurst believes "he is real but everyone else is unreal." That includes the teacher he killed, John Gilette, who in Wurst's mind "was already dead or unreal." Wurst told Sadoff that, excepting himself, everyone has been programmed by the government by means of "time tablets" that control people's thoughts.

There are other kids lost in their own worlds. Trickey, according to a report of the Oklahoma Office of Juvenile Affairs, "does not show any remorse for his crime and has little insight into his problems." Father John Kiernan, who used to visit Solomon regularly, says he seemed unaware of the consequences of his rampage. But in 1999, Solomon carved an X across his chest, apparently with a fingernail, and last January he attempted suicide by swallowing 22 pills of the antidepressant Elavil that he had bought from another inmate.

Many years will pass before most of the shooters come up for possible release. Three of them expect never to be paroled. Others will be men of 50 or even 70 before they have that option. But a handful of these boys, sentenced in more lenient states, will be released during the next five to seven years. Trickey's continued detention is reviewed every six months, and he will certainly go free by the time he turns 19. Cordova gets out at age 21. So do Johnson and Golden.

For his part, Solomon is in for 40 years. He's likely to be haunted by nightmares for much of that duration. "I've been having dreams and many flashbacks, and most recently, I have been hearing screams," he wrote after his arrest. "I know that it's just in my mind, [but] it's like I'm really hearing them, as if someone were screaming in my face. Usually when it's time to go to sleep and everything is quiet is when my thoughts get worst, because it's all I can hear." Of a dream, he said, "I see myself standing there, shooting me." In his sleep, he is his own victim. And when he wakes up, he is too.

I SHOULD HAVE SPOKEN UP

Josh Stevens, as told to Stephanie Booth

On March 5, 2001, Andy Williams killed two students and injured thirteen more in the halls of Santana High School in Santee, California. Before his shooting spree, Williams had confided his plans several times to friends who failed to take him seriously. Josh Stevens was one of those friends. In the following selection, Stevens expresses his deep regret that he did nothing to stop Andy Williams. The devastating guilt led him to turn to drugs shortly after the Santee shootings, he confesses, and he ended up in trouble with the law himself. Now a spokesperson for PAX, an organization working to end gun violence, Stevens advises students to tell someone if they hear a friend threaten to commit a school shooting. Stephanie Booth is a freelance writer who contributes frequently to *Teen People, Cosmopolitan,* and *Seventeen.*

In February 2001, I was walking home from school when my friend Andy Williams suddenly said, "I wanna pull a Columbine." He'd had a really bad day—a teacher had embarrassed him in front of the class—and I thought he was kidding. "All right, Andy," I joked.

Like me, Andy was a ninth-grader at Santana High School in Santee, Calif. We hung out at the local skate park and got to be great friends. We both liked punk and heavy metal, and we both played bass guitar. Andy was hilarious, but looking back, I can see he struggled with depression. He'd moved to California from Maryland and was having a hard time fitting in because he wasn't tough like other kids in our neighborhood.

We Thought He Was Just Kidding

I dismissed Andy's "Columbine" comment until two days later when a bunch of us were just hanging out. From nowhere, Andy suddenly said he wanted to take a gun and shoot people in the school hallway. One girl made him promise he wouldn't. "OK, I promise," Andy said, smiling. But several days later, he asked me and another friend if we wanted to get guns and do "it" with him. We were like, "No! Are you serious?" He said he was kidding.

On Monday, March 5, 2001, just before 9:30 A.M., a friend banged on my bedroom window and yelled, "Andy did it!" I got dressed and ran the three blocks to school. The campus was total chaos: people running everywhere, police cars and ambulances with their lights flashing. Andy had taken his dad's .22-caliber revolver and randomly sprayed bullets in a bathroom and hallway. Thirteen people had been injured and two others had been killed.

The police questioned me for eight hours. Word spread that Andy had told me about his plans and [that] I'd done nothing to stop him. The school district refused to let me come back to school, and it suddenly seemed like every student was out to kick my butt. People even called me at home to threaten me. It got to the point where I just stayed home and slept all the time.

No Way to Escape the Past

Nobody wants to be a rat, but you have to tell someone if one of your friends threatens violence. My best friend is in jail and two people lost their lives, and that will always hang over my head. In the weeks after, I started hanging out with a group of druggies—I think as a way to escape what had happened and how I might have prevented it. Before long, I was arrested for drug possession. The judge sentenced me to six months in a residential treatment center, where I am now [in 2002]. I honestly don't think any of this would have happened if not for the shooting.

I'll be here until February, and then I plan to finish school. I've also become a spokesperson for Pax, an organization that helps prevent gun violence. I don't want another school shooting to happen, and nobody should go through what I did. If I could do things over, I would have personally gone to Andy's house and told his father what was going on.

School Bullies Drove My Son to Suicide

Gabi Clayton

In the following selection, Gabi Clayton relates the story of her son, Bill, who came out as a bisexual while he was attending Olympia High School in Washington. As Clayton reveals, her son was a frequent target of homophobic harassment during his high school years. However, he did not hesitate to get involved when a controversy over gay rights erupted in his school in the spring of 1995. Shortly after Bill made a public appearance in support of gay rights at a school board meeting, he was brutally attacked and beaten in the high school parking lot. A month later, Bill committed suicide—an act that Clayton believes stemmed from the trauma of the assault and from Bill's inability to feel safe as a bisexual teen. Clayton is a licensed mental health counselor and the cofounder of Families United Against Hate, which provides assistance to victims of hate crimes.

Bill came out to us as bisexual when he was 14. He was afraid to tell us, because he knew that other kids had told their parents and that their parents had disowned them or reacted in other ways that were frightening. He had read the book I had loaned him, *Changing Bodies, Changing Lives*, and there were coming-out stories in the book. Finally he worked up the courage to tell us and we assured him that we loved him and accepted him. He was so happy that he wanted to tell the whole world. We recommended a support group out at the college which I had just graduated from. Bill went to that group three times and stopped—he said he really liked it but that he was fine and didn't need to go any more.

The Kid I Knew and Loved

Bill was the child who came home from school the first week in first grade *so* excited because his teacher had let him go to a special room! Turns out he finished a project early and decided to make animal noises to entertain the other children. As discipline he was sent to the coat room off the classroom. He enjoyed swinging on the closet bar so much that he wondered if the teacher would let him do it again the next day.

He was a gifted student who didn't always get the best of grades because he was always doing twenty things at the same time—and homework wasn't always on the top of the list.

Shy? Well, he told me that he was shy, but it was really hard to tell. His friends always loved him—when he wasn't driving them crazy.

He wanted to be a sculptor, a teacher, an architect, a counselor. . . .

An Assault

So, he told us he went to that support group three times, and we didn't question it. Over the next year he had a hard time in school, but seemed basically OK—sometimes somewhat withdrawn or moody. We were worried, but thought it was just typical teen emotional ups and downs. We were wrong.

On the way to the third support group meeting, he had met a man from the group who was 20 years old and who told Bill he was a member of another support group for gay/lesbian/bisexual/transgendered youth. He talked Bill into getting off the bus to go to his house "to borrow a book." When they got there he made Bill have sex with him. Bill was only a 14-year-old kid who didn't expect this, didn't know what to do, and he was unable to stop it. He came home that day and pretended he had gone to that meeting because he didn't want to admit to anyone—especially himself—what had happened. Ironically perhaps, at the time I was doing a graduate internship at a counseling center that specializes in sexual abuse.

Bill finally told Sam, his best friend. He told Sam that the memories of that sexual assault were overwhelming him and that he was suicidal. He asked Sam not to tell anyone, but Sam put the friendship on the line and told me, because he didn't want to lose his friend. Bill was relieved once we knew, and we reported it to the police and got Bill started with a therapist.

It took the police a long time to find the man. When they finally questioned him he confessed to exactly what Bill had said. Then he got a lawyer, pled not guilty at his arraignment, and managed to avoid jail and court until a month *after* Bill died. (He finally went to prison for 13 months.) So, Bill would see him around town—which aggravated the post-traumatic stress he was in counseling for. There were times when Bill would suddenly take a nose dive into severe depression for no apparent reason. Later we would find out that it was because he had seen this man on the bus or at the movies. Bill was so depressed and suicidal at one point that he spent some time in the hospital.

He stayed in counseling, and finally was getting back to being his old, impish self again. His mental health improved tremendously. He had a summer job doing computer and office stuff, and he loved it. He started looking forward to school again (after two rough years),

and he felt like he had a future. Yes, he was back! He and his counselor agreed that he was done with therapy, and she closed his case
with Crime Victims Compensation—on April 5th, 1995.

The Beginning of the End

The Activist Club at Olympia High School had invited Colonel Mar-
garethe Cammermeyer to speak at a school assembly in honor of
Women's History Month. (She is the highest ranking person to have
challenged the military's ban of gays, and was the subject of the TV
movie *Serving in Silence*.)

Controversy erupted when a group of homophobic parents and
community members—mostly people who object to homosexuality
on "religious grounds"—found out that she had accepted the invita-
tion and that the assembly was scheduled. We (supporters) found out
that there was going to be a hullabaloo at the next school board meeting, and that these people were going to attend in large numbers to
complain and ask the school board to cancel the assembly. Bill was
out at school, and he was one of a group of kids who put up flyers
about the assembly and promoted people attending the school board
meeting to support the speech.

Catherine (our housemate and our kid's second mom) and I and
Bill and many others attended. All in all there were about three hun-
dred people there and the meeting lasted for about two and a half
hours. I think there were a few more supporters than objectors who
spoke—I was one of them. The school board decided to remain firm
in their decision to let her speak, and she did—on March 21, 1995.
But the climate in the community was not good during this time.
There were some awful, hateful letters to the editor in our daily newspaper, and in general a lot of anti-gay feelings were stirred up.

April 6, 1995

On April 6, 1995, Sam and his girlfriend, Jenny, were walking with Bill
near their high school to Jenny's house to watch a video they had
rented. Four guys—one of whom knew Bill and Sam because he was in
the same high school (and had gone to their middle school before
that)—followed them in a car and yelled things I will not repeat related
to sexual orientation. Bill and his friends ignored them and decided to
walk through the high school campus, thinking it would be safer
because the gate was closed. The four guys drove off, but they parked
the car nearby, because the next thing Bill and his friends knew, they
came up on foot and surrounded them. They said "You wanna fight?"
Bill, Sam and Jenny tried to walk away—they didn't want to fight at all.

The four then brutally assaulted Bill and Sam, kicking and beating
them both into unconsciousness while Jenny screamed at them to
stop. It was broad daylight during Spring break.

When they regained consciousness a minute after the attackers left,

Bill, Sam and Jenny ran to the school custodian's office and called the police and then their families. They were taken to the emergency room where we met them. Bill had abrasions and bruises. They thought he might have kidney damage, but he didn't. Sam was a mess too, with a broken nose and many bruises.

While we were in the emergency room, one of the guys who did the assault came casually walking through with two other friends, to visit a friend who had just had a baby. Sam saw him and Sam's parents called the police. When they found him he confessed and told the police who the other guys were—they were all under 18 years old. The police treated it as a hate crime from the very beginning.

A Rally Against Hate

A lot of wonderful people in Olympia responded quickly and supported Bill (and us all) and held an incredible anti-hate crime rally on April 14th, a few days after the assault. Many people spoke there, including Colonel Cammermeyer, who returned to support the kids.

At the rally, Bill spoke from his heart. He said:

> In all likelihood, my friends Sam and Jenny will never have to tolerate this—or never have to endure this type of hate crime or any other type in their lives—and I hope that's true. But as an openly bisexual person in Olympia, I'm probably—or may be—the victim of this sort of thing again. Hate crimes—especially those against homosexuals and bisexuals and transgendered people—are on the rise in this area. And that is why now—more than ever—we, the gay community, need to come out and band together and fight for our civil rights and our right to be safe in our homes and on the streets. Thank you for coming."

I spoke to Bill—and to all the people who were there in Sylvester Park that day. I stood at the microphone (voice and hands shaking—I am not comfortable with making speeches) and I said:

> First of all I felt it was important as Bill's mom for me to stand up here and tell Bill how very much I love him and how incredibly proud I am of him. And I'm incredibly proud of him not just for the courage he's showing tonight and since this happened, but because of who he is as a person—and that means every bit of him including the fact that he is bisexual. I think it's important for parents to do that. . . .

> My father was a German Jewish refugee, and the hate he faced as a child in Germany is the same hate that my son and these kids faced on that street by that school. And hate doesn't grow in a vacuum. It can't grow unless we allow it to. It grows on fear and it grows on silence."

Alec (my husband and Bill's dad, who had always been the one of us who handled public speaking with more ease) stepped up to the microphone and said:

> I had a speech planned—but this outpouring of sympathy and support has got me all choked up. I can't talk—thank you for coming.

Alec was in tears as he left the podium.

Bill's older brother Noel was in college and was unable to come home until after the rally in Sylvester Park. But he sent this letter to the editor of the *Olympian* (our daily newspaper). It was published on April 22.

> My name is Noel Clayton. On April 6 my brother, Bill, and his friends were assaulted at Olympia High School.
>
> I just wanted to write to extend my thanks to a number of people whose support has been invaluable in this crisis.
>
> Not least among these is *The Olympian* staff members who have treated the victims with dignity and respect despite those in the area who would like to silence or ignore gay-bashing as a problem.
>
> I would like to thank the Olympia Police Department and the prosecutor's office who have worked hard and carefully to make sure that the boys who were responsible are brought to justice.
>
> Also I would like to thank the 200 to 300 people who showed up at the rally to support Bill and Sam, as well as those, like myself who were not able to make it but were there in spirit.
>
> Finally I would like to remind everyone that this is not over.
>
> Our families will be dealing with the effects of this assault for years to come, if not for the rest of our lives.
>
> I will never forget the events of these past weeks. I intend to fight, and I ask you all to join me, until no one has to walk the streets afraid, until no one has to live in fear of persecution or assault no matter what their race, religion or sexuality.

The Consequences of Hate

We thought he was going to make it—he seemed to handle things really well until after the rally, and then he crashed back into depression. He was suicidal again—it was too much. The assault sent him right back into the place he had fought so hard to get out of. He suddenly became depressed and suicidal, and we had to put him in the hospital again. While he was in the hospital he heard that a friend of his was gay-bashed at school in a nearby town.

After about 10 days he came home. We and his doctors in the hospital thought he had gotten past being suicidal. But Bill took a massive overdose on May 8th. Alec found him unconscious on the kitchen floor and had him rushed to the hospital, but they couldn't save him.

He didn't leave a suicide note, but he had said to me before he was hospitalized after the rally that he was just tired of coping. It was the constant knowledge that at any time he could be attacked again simply because of who he was, that at any time his friends could be attacked for the same reason, that despite the love of his family and friends all he could see ahead was a lifetime of facing a world filled with hate and violence, going from one assault to another. He was 17 years old—an age when kids are supposed to be excited about moving out into the world as adults. The only place he felt safe was at home. He saw no hope, so he chose to end his life.

The memorial service we held for Bill was an incredible part of our healing process. It was a big job to put it all together. We felt it had to be something Bill would have wanted—and he had considered himself a pagan. We felt so strongly that he had to be respected in this last thing. It was an incredible ceremony—so many people helped, and so many friends and strangers came—we had let it be known that anyone in the community who wanted to come was invited. There was music and drumming and ceremony and people who wished to were given a chance to speak. . . .

Everyone there had been asked to bring a candle, and was given a prayer stick (a small twig) to hold during the memorial and asked to think of good wishes for Bill. After the ceremony we stood at the door and lit each person's candle. Each person took their candle over to Sylvester Park (which was just across the street) in silent vigil, and there we collected the sticks. Later that night family and a few close friends took the baskets of sticks to the land behind Sam's house and placed each stick in a beautiful bonfire to release the wishes for Bill so that they would travel with him. It was wonderful. Not at all "traditional"—but then we have never been known for being that.

Pouring Salt into the Wound

Right after Bill died, a coroner talked to us—and asked us if we would allow him to be an organ donor. We said yes, and she talked to us for a while and asked some questions. She already knew about the hate crime. When she indicated that there might be a problem and she would get back to us, we thought it was because of the overdose.

Then (I can't remember how long later—time was a mess those days) we got a call from her. Bill could not be an organ donor—the Lions Eye Bank had turned down the donation because of his sexual orientation—he was in a high risk group!!!! I couldn't believe it. I told the coroner how angry and upset this made me.

After that I received a letter from the Lions, explaining that they were "not able to honor the donation of tissue from any member of this at risk population because of the possibility of transmitting HIV to a recipient" and "Although Bill was probably HIV negative, the possibility does exist that he could have been exposed but would not test positive. I hope you understand that such a risk is too large for us to take."

And I wrote back on June 12, 1995:

> It has taken me some time to respond to your letter. In it you explained that the Lions Eye Bank would not accept my son as a donor because he was openly bisexual, and therefore a member of a high risk population. It is somehow ironic that Bill had an eye operation when he was younger which was paid for by the Lions Club in Mississippi.

> Bill committed suicide at age 17, after being assaulted in a hate crime because he was bisexual. Frankly, reading your rejection and justification was one of the most difficult things I have had to face since his death. In your words I saw what my son decided he could not face in the world every day—all the homophobia, hatred and fear of who he was as a person.

> Just who is it that you believe is safe? Heterosexuals? Married persons? Children? In my work as a mental health therapist, I work with young children who are at risk of HIV from sexual abuse. WHO IS SAFE? Open your eyes. You are in total denial if you believe that you are protecting people with this policy.

> If the reason you rejected Bill's corneal tissue was because of the sexual assault which I had discussed with [the coroner], it happened when he was 14 years old. He was tested for HIV over a year later—much later than the six month window you mentioned. But no one took the time to find out the particulars—just a flat denial based on his being bisexual.

> I am also shocked that a group who is using the facilities at a state funded hospital is able to do so with such blatantly discriminatory policies.

> I am assuming that you were not stating your own personal beliefs in the letter, but the policy of the Lions Eye Bank. This makes it no easier. Institutional intolerance and discrimination are VERY personal. And institutions are made up of individual persons. If you do not agree with this policy, I urge you to help change it.

> Silence is where the hate grows that killed my son.

At the end of July I received another letter from them, explaining that as a certified member of the EBAA [Eye Bank Association of America] they must adhere to medical standards established by a national medical advisory committee, with recommendations from the Centers for Disease Control (CDC). They hoped I would understand that they had no choice but to decline the donation because the decision was based on national regulations. . . .

There was a phone call later to see if I was still upset. They tried to get me to "understand" and I just wouldn't. Wrong is wrong.

The boys who assaulted Bill and Sam were finally sentenced to 20–30 days in juvenile detention followed by probation and community service and 4 hours of diversity training focusing on sexual orientation.

Missed, but Not Forgotten

Bill's life and death has touched perhaps thousands of people. There was an outpouring of support for us here—both from friends and from people we had never met. Throughout the time of the hate crime and Bill's suicide I have never felt so supported and connected to a community.

At the memorial for Bill I was given a letter written by Gery Gerst—Bill's History teacher at Olympia High School that year, who was unable to attend. In his letter he said:

Bill was such a caring person, a sharer. He gave so much to me during lunch or before school. In class he shared insights that no one else did; what a big heart, gentle man, probing mind . . . in the time he was to be on this earth he touched so many lives in so many positive ways, especially mine. I want to tell you parents that both your sons have been kind, caring, giving, and considerate to me and I value that so much. In this world that is a tremendous legacy.

Clearly, as you can see by the turnout of support at Sylvester Park and now, Bill was and is loved. Fear not that he will be forgotten. Missed he will be, but not forgotten. . . .

I'd like to write to Bill, now, what I would have written in his annual:

Bill, you have impressed me with your keen insights into history, government, and people. Your insight comes from deep caring and feeling, the result of being tested of character and perseverance. The world is lucky to have such as you for your demeanor is gentle and your dedication to truth and learning is exemplary. My class won't be the same without your original additions to discussions and your sharings with me after class. Your brain was always working, and so was your heart. Thanks for help with "the" assembly and for your trust and confidence in me, not to mention your smile that showed you cared. You are going to be missed, but the door's always open . . . drop by some time and know your time this year was valued.

Nothing will bring Bill back. I am sharing his story in the hope that it can help in some way to put an end to the hate and homophobia. This world cannot remain so hard to live in and to have hope in—not for all the "Bill's" who are out there now, and all who are yet to come.

Last Words

Alec read "Bill's Story" and asked me to include this:

After Bill's death I found in one of his notebooks where he had drawn the gay symbol, a pink triangle. Across it he had written, "This is not my choice. This is not forced upon me. This just is."

We wanted to create some kind of memorial to Bill, and without making a conscious decision we realized that the best memorial we could create would be our own lives—working towards the elimination of the senseless and destructive hatred that is all too prevalent in our society. Of those who may be touched by Bill's story we ask one thing: join us.

CONFESSIONS OF A VIOLENT MOVIE WRITER

William Mastrosimone

In the following essay, screenwriter William Mastrosimone describes his personal odyssey in exploring the connection between
Hollywood violence and school shootings. Mastrosimone explains
that some of his movie scripts have featured graphic violence. As
incidents of school violence increasingly made newspaper headlines during the 1990s, he began to question his contribution to
Hollywood's emphasis on blood and guts, especially in movies
that attract teenage audiences. He was also appalled by the entertainment industry's failure to take responsibility for the trend
toward gratuitous media violence and its potential effects on vul-
nerable children and teenagers. He wrote a play entitled, *Bang
Bang You're Dead*. The play became a TV movie by the same title
and was the winner of five Emmy Awards and the Peabody Award.

Sitting at *Natural Born Killers* in a packed house, kids cheered every
shot, stab, kick. They weren't seeing social commentary. They were
drunken Roman citizens watching humans thrown to the beasts in
the Colosseum. A short time later, sitting at *Pulp Fiction*, they rolled in
the aisles when the gun went off accidentally and the kid was killed
in the back seat of the car, fouling the upholstery. They weren't seeing
black comedy. They were loving the total freedom of these two men
to rove about with guns, killing for fun. Something snapped in me
back then in '94 and I began to feel a sense of shame about belonging
to the Hollywood community. And those movies were tame compared to others. But for me a saturation point had been reached. A
line was crossed between artistry and social responsibility.

Those feelings of shame grew into a play entitled *Like Totally
Weird*, and then a screenplay by the same title. In the course of
rewriting it, school shootings began in towns across America: Moses
Lake, Bethel, Pearl, Paducah, Jonesboro, Edinboro, Pomona, Fayet-
teville, Onalaska, Springfield. A plague of kids killing kids in unlikely
places spread over the country. I began to collect newspaper articles
to study the killers. One thing became clear: these kids were not psy-

William Mastrosimone, "Confessions of a Violent Movie Writer," *Written By*,
June/July 1999. Copyright © 1999 by *Written By*, the Magazine of the Writers Guild
of America. Reproduced by permission.

chotics. They were normal kids living *our* fantasies.

Three days after the Springfield [Oregon] killing in '98, as my family sat around the dinner table, one of my kids casually mentioned that upon entering English class, he and his friends saw that someone had written on the blackboard: "I'm going to kill everyone in this class. And the teacher, too." The blackboard phantom was soon discovered and suspended, but peace of mind in our sleepy little town in the foothills of Mt. Rainier was hard to come by. Like other parents, my wife and I realized that our kids are no longer safe, and that even though the blackboard phantom said it was all a joke, we understood that he was imitating another fantasy similiar to that of the Paducah killer who imitated a movie. The Jonesboro killers were obviously acting out some kind of military fantasy. Sadly, it became eminently reasonable to assume there is a potential killer in every school.

The potential kid killer lives in isolation, in a state where realities are distorted and exaggerated. His most potent fantasy is that of revenge on those who reject him. He looks for ways to sustain his fantasy, for a jump-start of his imagination. Movies, video games, Marilyn Manson do just fine.

Violence Is Violence

I made lots of high-minded excuses for myself that night. A man attempts to rape a woman and is thrown into a fireplace and tortured by her in *Extremities*. In *The Beast*, a Soviet tank is used to execute a rebel. In *The Burning Season* [cowritten], a man is set on fire and his Amazonian village forced to watch. I would like to think that my brand of violence is justified. But maybe the potential killer makes no fine distinction. Maybe violence is violence is violence. Maybe in looking for answers to alleviate his pain of being a "nobody," he takes his movie idol as a role model, merging life and art.

It was then I began to see that my shame was an epiphany about the pervasive and profound effect we writers have on the world. It was then that my shame became a pain in the pit of my stomach. Like Oedipus, I had been seeking the cause of the plague upon my land, not knowing that the culprit was myself.

Unable to sleep that night, playwright Arthur Miller's words kept going through my head: "Tragedy is a play about the chickens coming home to roost." America's chickens had come home to roost. Inevitably, hubris triggers Nemesis. By morning, I had the first draft of a play entitled *Bang Bang You're Dead*, intended to be performed by school kids as a tool for students to confront the potential killer in the audience. I brought it to the attention of Springfield drama teacher Mike Fisher. He brought it to his students who had been in the cafeteria when bullets began flying. Some of them were wounded.

Thus began an odyssey that has changed me forever. We quietly rehearsed during the mostly peaceful year, launching our world premiere in Eugene, Oregon, at which time we announced that the play would be posted on the Internet royalty-free for any student production.

A week later, Littleton happened. Five weeks later, Heritage High School in Georgia happened.

Hollywood Is in Denial

I was not surprised by Littleton. But I was nauseated by Hollywood's knee-jerk state of denial. A reporter from the *Los Angeles Times* told me that he could not find one writer in all of Hollywood to talk about violence. Wave after wave of copycat bomb threats closed hundreds of schools across the country. Another body dropped in a Canadian school. Kids in trenchcoats seemed to multiply. A sixth-grade boy shot three kids on the playground with a BB gun. Lawsuits were pointing the sword of blind Justice at Hollywood. Amid such madness, the purveyors of fantasy get a sudden case of laryngitis. We heard from the apologists but not the greenlight people.

Hollywood silence has become strident.

Hollywood extremists say we have no responsibility. Outside extremists say that it's all our fault. I myself am looking for the truth between those indefensible positions. And there are hundreds of laboratory and real-life studies that have to give pause to any writer with a functioning conscience. These studies are not theories. They are scientific fact. Like it or not, there is a correlation between violent entertainment and violent behavior. The evidence is overwhelming that increased viewing of violence leads to increased acceptance of aggressive behavior.

No, a movie does not make a kid go out and kill; but the accumulation of violent entertainment over a span of years predisposes a kid to be indifferent to violence against others, and to see violence as a first, not a last, resort.

Lt. Col. Dave Grossman has shown that violent video games made the Paducah killer a world-class marksman, even though he never fired a real gun until the day he walked into school and killed three girls.

There's a new video game out. The advertising goes: "Kill your friends without guilt." The package allows you to scan your yearbook into your computer and morph the heads of your friends and enemies onto the video targets. Anybody want to defend this game?

The debate is over.

A Call to Conscience

If, as writers, we are not convinced that the post-Littleton copycat bomb threats reveal our movie audience to be filled with troubled kids looking for inspiration, we are either mindless or heartless. If conscience is not part of our product, then we are no different than the cigarette companies who lied for decades that there is no cause and effect between smoke and cancer. We might also be compared to the gun manufacturers who proclaim that 98 percent of people who own guns don't commit crimes or kill anyone. Many in Hollywood echo the National Rifle Association defense, that most people who watch violent movies don't go on rampages.

As the intelligentsia, we have a responsibility. Those who think that to hold back would cramp their style should note that some of the best movies ever made were spawned under Hayes Office censorship. If Alfred Hitchcock felt straitjacketed, he never let on. We are all bound by a social contract wherein we agree to stop at red lights, if not to safeguard other lives, then for our own survival. Some of our own are speeding through the red lights, drunk on the freedom and benefits of The Biz, leaving a trail of dead kids behind.

If we continue to ignore the possibility that we may be part of the lethal alchemy of kids killing kids, if we continue to pander to the worst instincts and call it "holding a mirror up to society," if we continue to devalue human life and call it "First Amendment rights," we shall reap the whirlwind, feel a public backlash, and see our freedoms curtailed. We will be known to history as the sell-out generation. Hollywood will stand for the Roman Colosseum, a horror chamber where endless ways of killing were invented to please packed audiences, and we will come to foretell the fall of an empire.

Who's to Blame?

I apportion blame everywhere:

Kids must treat everyone politely, no matter how freaky. (The Littleton killers said, "This is what you get for the way you treated us.")

Parents must learn from the Paducah parents of murdered kids: "Love your kids enough to find out what's going on in their lives. Love them enough to say no to them."

Schools must set up anonymous tip lines so harassment by or of freaks can be reported.

The media must remember that, to a troubled mind, any publicity is good publicity, and then do what the *Chicago Sun-Times* did: report Littleton but bury it in the back pages, thus depriving the unknown wannabe of the attention he craves.

The President must treat this matter as if there were a terrorist organization roaming the country killing kids at random. He must understand that kids are the country's greatest self-interest, and prosecute this cause with the same energy and determination that is shown in dropping bombs on far-flung places. The President should enlist the best and brightest minds and give this matter the same urgency of the Manhattan Project and demand a solution on his desk by September 1.

Hollywood and corporate America must search their souls. Get out of your ivory tower and acknowledge you are part of a society. Stop seeing kids as an income. Kids today are the most exploited generation in history, not in body, but in mind and spirit. The science of demographics knows how to manipulate the levers of the psyche to move masses of people. There is a core of writers, producers, and actors who are traffickers in gratuitous violence—the crack dealers of fantasy—who feel they must "push the envelope," as they say.

I offer this litmus test: If an act of violence is without remorse or consequences and uses human suffering for "entertainment," it's wrong. No troubled kid who sees *Saving Private Ryan* finds inspiration to go out and kill; he sees people sacrificing their lives for a greater good. What can you say of Freddy and Jason? We must balance our rights with the right of kids to die of natural causes.

We can still explore the human condition. The subject matter need not change; only our techniques have to change. If we are not willing to make that sacrifice, we are no better than that creep who walked away when he saw his best friend molest and murder that young girl in a Nevada casino. It's going to take key people to reverse the trend, but first it's going to take those of us on the bottom of the totem pole to put our scripts where our consciences are and refuse to be a tool of the exploiters among us.

Focus off the Academy Awards, and focus on the Humanitas Awards, Hollywood's only real claim to a soul. (When I attended the Humanitas Award ceremony [in 1995], there was not one reporter, not one camera, no one to comment on my new necktie.)

Some of our own feel blameless because they feel no shame. I say they're beyond the pale.

I have come to this point after a five-year journey, from feeling ashamed of my profession while watching movies, to the world premiere of *Bang Bang You're Dead* when I, as a Hollywood writer, came face-to-face with parents who lost kids to violence in Bethel, Alaska . . . Jonesboro, Arkansas . . . Paducah, Kentucky . . . Springfield, Oregon. . . . All words failed me in a crowded lobby when the father of a boy who still had a bullet in his spine poked a finger in my chest and said, "'Bout time you people caught on."

I do not regret the course I have taken. At bottom, it's a spiritual battle between exploiters and nurturers of kids, between the elitist mentality and those of us who feel we're all connected, and that we as artists are part of—not on top of—society. I have turned down work that I deemed unworthy. I will probably lose more work for speaking my mind. But what I have, along with Mike Fisher and the Springfield High School kids, is the knowledge that our play has been downloaded 10,000 times from the Web site, and that many of those downloads will turn into thousands of shoestring school productions. We also have the testimony of a girl in Eugene who came backstage with a tear-streaked face to tell us that she had made up her mind to kill herself, but seeing the play made her believe in life once more, and she thanked us all for saving her life. That's a story I can take home to my kids. Or anybody else's kids. And that's what matters to me now.

Isolation Hurts: The Perspective of a Teen-Novel Writer

Chris Crutcher

The author of several novels for young adults, Chris Crutcher has worked with children and adolescents as a teacher, principal, and family therapist. In the following selection, he discusses the impact of school violence on his work. During the 1990s, Crutcher explains, he wrote a novel that included a fictionalized school shooting, but after the 1999 Columbine massacre, he decided to withdraw his manuscript from publication. At the same time, he noticed a change in the education field, as many school districts began to look with suspicion on alienated students. Crutcher maintains that this trend is misguided because it only serves to further isolate the very students who are already lonely and confused. In his presentations at teachers' conferences and university classrooms, he urges educators to reach out to these students who desperately need to feel accepted and included.

If Columbine and similar tragedies have taught us anything about teens, it is the value of belonging and the danger of isolation.

Trashing My Novel

A minor casualty of the 1999 Columbine tragedy was a coming-of-age novel I had recently finished. The story included a fictionalized school shooting loosely based on one in Moses Lake, WA, [in February 1996]. In what I believe to be the granddaddy of these modern shootings, a 14-year-old boy named Barry Loukaitis walked into his afternoon math class, wearing boots, a cowboy hat, and a long-rider's coat, which concealed a rifle and two pistols. He first shot and killed the boy he considered his major tormentor, the teacher, another classmate, and wounded at least one other student. He then demanded that everyone line up in the back of the room; his intent, to shoot them one by one.

A teacher/coach was able to get into the room, and after a truly terrifying exchange that could easily have ended his life, captured the gun to end the carnage. Subsequent news accounts recorded quick calls for forgiveness of the gunman juxtaposed with cries for an adult trial: responses that became familiar in the following months and years as we watched footage from Pearl, MS, Paducah, KY, Jonesboro, AR, Springfield, OR, and points beyond. At the time I began writing my novel, however, none of those towns was famous in that Barry Loukaitis way. I believed I was writing about an anomaly, the kind of event that would allow me to highlight the humiliation and rage many outsiders feel. But as each new shooting occurred, I read more newspaper accounts of the culprits' backgrounds—along with accounts of community, school, and legal responses—looking for new truths that could make my story authentic. Let me say, it is not helpful to my process of writing fiction to check my material daily with CNN.

I took more time to finish the novel than I anticipated, but finally got it in the mail about two weeks before I was to make a presentation to the Texas Library Association. I arrived in Dallas, took a cab to my hotel, unpacked my clothes, and flipped on the television set, only to be astonished with the rest of the nation by the now familiar images of students hurrying out of Columbine with their hands on their heads, past the police and SWAT teams. When I recovered from the initial shock, the obvious became just that, and I called Susan Hirschman, then my editor at Greenwillow Books. She said, "We've been waiting for your call." I asked if my manuscript was on her desk and she said yes.

"Is your garbage can next to your desk?"

She said yes, and I said, "Do it."

She said, "Thank you."

There was no way that novel could have been published without being seen as exploitative, no way my intent would break through. Absent that, Columbine still reduced the events in my story to a footnote, our collective consciousness regarding guns in schools forever changed.

The Crisis Creates a New Demand

Even with several years' work down the drain, my financial future was not threatened because I could have brought my very part-time, private child and family therapy practice to full speed in less than a week. Every student who wore a long, dark coat or employed forefinger and thumb to mimic a barrel and hammer or used "Columbine" as a verb was suddenly suspect, often suspended, and in many instances required to take a psychological examination in order to reenter school. Had the ACLU [American Civil Liberties Union] been listed on the New York Stock Exchange, I'd have mortgaged my house to buy every share I could get my hands on. Schools didn't even know what they wanted evaluated. They were asking the psychological community to do the impossible, to tell them which students were likely to come to school with guns a-blazing.

While I understand the panicky reaction we had as a culture to the rash of shooting—it was a smaller version of the kind of thinking that led us to put Japanese-American citizens into concentration camps during World War II—it couldn't have been less helpful. If these shootings have taught us anything, it is the value of belonging and, conversely, the damage of isolation. With the exception of the few who have turned out to be clinically mentally ill, the shooters have mostly been kids who existed on the outside, who felt profoundly uncared for. They were, in their own perceptions, teased, dismissed, humiliated. Far too often, our tendency as adults is to be dismissive: "If you're feeling bad, you need to tell someone," we say, or "You don't have to be on the outside, there are things you can do to be more popular." Then, we tend to become frustrated and irritated when they don't follow our simplistic advice. What we often fail to understand in teens is something we often fail to understand in ourselves: that when any human drops below a certain level of self-worth, nothing matters. Sometimes the personal response to that sense of worthlessness is, "Woe be unto somebody when I don't care anymore." I read a quote in a weekly newsmagazine from a man on death row not long after the Columbine incident. His quote ought to be a bumper sticker. He said, "I'd rather be wanted for murder than not be wanted at all."

Educating Future Teachers

I visit the adolescent literature classes at a local university one time per quarter to talk about my books and about the troubled kids I sometimes write about. I make myself available for those presentations because I am constantly struck, as I sit across my office from some teenager telling his horror story, that this kid is in a class in a school somewhere in town, dealing with the things he's telling me—at the same time a teacher is trying to help him learn math or English or social studies, and that teacher can't have a clue that maybe her kindness or attention is creating such anxiety that the student will be compelled to respond negatively to it. The student knows one thing about kindness, or any other "good thing" happening in his life. He knows, from experience, that it turns bad. And while he can't control that "truth," he can control when, and when the anxiety becomes intolerable, he takes control, often blowing up. So, a teacher who has been doing her best to make sure the student experiences her kindness, and the safety of her classroom, may become frustrated and irritated that her best efforts are not well received, and the struggle begins. The classroom becomes "not safe" for the student, becomes one more errant example of how the world turns on him, and another layer of self-contempt is laid down.

I described that basic self-destructive process to a class of college students within six months of graduating and taking over classrooms of their own. A young man said he'd been instructed regularly in his education courses to get control of his classes with an iron hand, then relax later as conditions allowed. He asked me if that was "wrong."

I said, "God, are they still saying that? I heard it first in 1964; walked into my first classroom in 1970 and discovered I didn't have an iron fist, and immediately considered myself a failure, as if I weren't cut out for teaching." While there is still some question regarding whether or not I was cut out for teaching (ask any student who took geography from me), that wasn't the reason. I went on to tell this student something else I believe to be true: that there is little in good teaching that doesn't hinge on relationship, and that taking time to establish structure while also inviting dialogue replaces the iron fist just fine, thank you. One way to do that is to look at the "structure" of the classroom as something that is made up of boundaries of physical and emotional safety, and of whatever rules one needs to get through the business of the day, which of course is education. Within that structure is where the relationship takes place.

Someone at a teacher's conference recently asked why I didn't take time to write a nonfiction book about dealing with adolescents. I thought about it briefly and realized I would begin with, "Don't judge and don't take it personally," and that would be pretty much the end of my book. Hard to charge $20 for that. We fail to remember sometimes that adolescence is, first and foremost, a developmental stage, that humans at that age are supposed to be separating, pushing away. The more solid the foundation we give them from which to push away, the better they will be able to trust that foundation, and turn to us when the pushing away gets too scary. At the same time, within that structure we need to begin the business of establishing relationship, which leads to mutual respect. We should be asking a lot of ourselves in this process: to not judge teenagers too harshly as they find their means of expression (because the vast majority really do want to find the pathway to responsible adulthood) and to not take their actions personally (because they aren't personal; the content is not as important as the process).

The Loneliness That Kills

At the same time, we can learn a great deal from the content if we listen. I was on the periphery of an 11-year-old's work in therapy recently. By coincidence he had lost a classmate in a suicide-homicide that was related to one of these school shootings. I had worked with his mother years ago, when he had been placed in foster care at age four because she had significantly abused and neglected him. In the end, his mother had chosen a man over her son and left him with his grandmother. His grandmother was (and is) a wonderful parent to him, but the loss of his mother remains an aching reminder of what it is not to be wanted—and much of his therapy has focused on his feelings of isolation. The boy is now overweight, has something of a speech impediment, and is picked on by classmates to the extent that he has chosen to be home-schooled.

He said something we all need to hear. He said, "We should have a loneliness building. We should get together a group of kids whose moms left them for drugs or bad guys, and they're lonely. Loneliness Group would be the name of the group. They would find out they all feel the same, then they don't have the feeling they are different. . . . The group would help people not hurt themselves too much. We should write a book called *Lonely People* and get money and build a building for lonely kids. Lonely grown-ups need their own building."

He went on to say that lonely kids try to find meaning, but they can't find it. "That's the loneliness that kills," he said. "People tease them and tease them and tease them until you can't take it any more. Then they hurt themselves or maybe other people."

Ending Isolation; Inviting Expression

I believe we have the knowledge to make our classrooms and school libraries places where loneliness simply is not allowed. Since the Columbine shootings, we have thrown large sums of money into providing security for our schools, and I have no problem with that. Many schools have also established inclusion activities for the kids who often can't find anything for themselves, which is definitely a step in the right direction. But we have also instituted a rash of zero-tolerance policies, which I do have a problem with, because the last thing we can afford for these kids is zero tolerance.

We should remember that the greatest portion of the disenfranchised kids at Columbine hit the deck, too, when the shooting started, that they were as astonished and traumatized as anyone else was. And we should also remember that in the days following that incident, outsiders all over the country stood up and identified themselves, because they now had a voice (ugly as it sometimes sounded). Instead of inviting those kids in, we tried to identify them and push them further out. Think of the number of times you have heard a parent say that some kid is a "bad influence" and that their child should stay away from him or her. Think of the number of times we have tried to break up groups of "undesirables." What arrogance it is to keep any children from finding a place to be included.

I think in the [time] since Columbine, we have learned some valuable lessons, but there are more to learn. If nothing else comes out of all this violence, we need to learn the importance of expression, how important it is for all of us to be heard and included.

At the end of my 11-year-old friend's conversation, he said in a very matter-of-fact, nonthreatening way, "I can see how a kid would come to school with a gun."

I want him to see how a kid wouldn't.

CHAPTER 4

PREVENTING SCHOOL VIOLENCE

CONFLICT RESOLUTION AND PEER MEDIATION

Stephen W. Smith and Ann P. Daunic

In the following article, Stephen W. Smith and Ann P. Daunic describe the use of conflict resolution and peer mediation programs to support positive behavior in schools. As Smith and Daunic explain, volunteer students are trained in conflict resolution techniques so that they can help their peers negotiate peaceful solutions to disputes. Although these programs require some adult supervision, they rely primarily on student leadership, giving young people the opportunity to work out problems among themselves in a responsible and nonviolent manner. Successful peer mediation programs prevent violence and teach students important interpersonal skills, the authors conclude. Smith is a professor of special education at the University of Florida in Gainesville. Daunic is a researcher at the University of Florida in Gainesville and a former school administrator, counselor, and tutor.

For years, professionals who work with school-aged children have been concerned about problems associated with destructively aggressive behavior. These problems are nothing new; however, school safety issues have become increasingly urgent with the recent occurrence of high-profile, violent events in schools across the country. School administrators continue to seek out procedures and programs that may reduce aggression among students and prevent serious incidents from occurring. Many traditional practices, such as detention or suspension, are often punitive and adult-directed, do not teach students positive conflict management, and do not have lasting effects. Consequently, researchers and school-based professionals have begun to advocate preventive approaches to behavior problems that combine student-centered, skill-building interventions with changes in the ecological context in which behaviors occur. Conflict resolution (CR) programs that incorporate peer mediation (PM) training exemplify such an approach. They have proliferated over the past decade and provide educators with an alternative to reactive, adult-directed strategies.

Definitions

Conflict resolution, as a school-based program, usually includes instruction to make conflict a constructive, rather than destructive, process. It is designed to be preventive. Conflict resolution concepts can be taught in self-contained units or infused within other academic content, and they can be taught to all students or to selected groups.

Peer mediation is an intervention, often used in conjunction with a conflict resolution curriculum, in which specially trained students follow specific procedures to help their peers negotiate a positive resolution to a conflict. While curriculum in conflict resolution is designed to teach students general concepts about positive approaches to conflict in daily life, peer mediation is a specific and formal opportunity for students to practice learned skills. Peer mediation may be taught to selected cadres of students who serve as mediators, or it can be a universal approach in which each student has an opportunity to act as a mediator on a rotating basis.

Peer mediation, as part of a conflict resolution program, is a significant move away from reactive, punitive, and seclusionary methods, and its proponents suggest that it can

- Provide students with a framework for resolving conflicts
- Give students an opportunity to assume responsibility for their own behavior
- Lower teachers' stress by reducing the number of student conflicts they have to handle
- Increase instructional time
- Help students understand how cultural diversity can affect interpersonal communication and human interactions

Teaching students to resolve their conflicts constructively can have positive effects on the school environment, particularly because students' chronic behavior problems demand considerable time and attention from teachers and administrative staff. Conflict resolution and peer mediation programs can focus not only on teaching students skills for managing conflict constructively, but also on creating environments that empower students and provide them opportunities to practice what they have learned. By developing a positive school approach to interpersonal conflict, teachers and administrators can help students develop the personal, social, and academic skills necessary for success in school and beyond. . . .

D.W. Johnson and R.T. Johnson argue that conflict, if managed constructively without violence, may be desirable. Conflict resolution and peer mediation are recommended procedures for addressing in positive ways the conflict that is inevitable in the schools.

Conflict Resolution

Conflict resolution programs typically include a curriculum designed to provide basic knowledge to students about individual differences, changing win-lose situations to win-win solutions and using negotiation to resolve conflicts effectively. A conflict resolution curriculum can focus on social skills such as empathy training, effective communication, and stress and anger management; attitudes about conflict; bias awareness; and/or negotiation and large-group problem solving. Teachers or other school professionals help students learn a process for handling interpersonal conflict by focusing on skill development within a general conceptual framework rather than on how to solve an immediate, specific problem. Students tend to view conflict situations as occasions in which there are winners and losers. Introducing them to scenarios where all parties can win offers a framework within which to view conflict as a learning opportunity to solve mutual problems and strengthen social relations. Conflict resolution curricula can introduce students to the productive aspects of conflict instead of focusing only on eliminating or preventing it. They may be especially effective when teachers use cooperative learning strategies to foster integrative, rather than competitive, approaches to learning.

Conflict resolution programs should be student- rather than adult-centered. Adults are not always available to help students negotiate solutions to their day-to-day conflicts. Programs that depend solely on adult decision making fail to teach students appropriate resolution skills to use in the absence of adult supervision. Through a variety of learning experiences, such as discussion, role plays, and simulations, and through a focus on student empowerment, conflict resolution curricula can (a) facilitate the understanding of conflict and its determinants, (b) teach students effective communication, problem solving, and negotiation, and (c) provide a foundation for education about peace and nonviolence.

Peer Mediation

Not only should adults teach students about conflict, they must also provide students with opportunities to practice what they learn in real-life conflict situations. Students are constantly exposed to violence and aggression in the media, often as win-lose situations, and they may be exposed to similar circumstances in their homes and communities. To counter the effects of such negative exposure, students need opportunities to observe appropriate, positive negotiations and to practice conflict resolution skills in unthreatening environments. Peer mediation, an explicit intervention in which students help their peers solve conflicts, offers such an opportunity. Mediation avoids an imposed adult solution and the resentment of authority that may come as a consequence of adult control. When mediators and disputants can work autonomously, school professionals are relieved of time-consuming attention to frequently occurring conflicts, and students are empowered to take responsibility for successfully resolving their disputes.

Peer mediation in the schools is conflict resolution conducted by and for students, allowing them a say in how their disputes will be resolved. It is a structured process consisting of specific steps student mediators use to help disputants define and solve a problem between them. As a significant part of an overall conflict resolution program, peer mediation can provide students with methods for resolving conflict peacefully and with skills to approach future conflict as a constructive opportunity. Peer mediation differs from other programs facilitated by peers, such as peer counselors or peer helpers, because it involves a clearly defined, formal process with distinct roles for each participant.

Schoolwide peer mediators are typically a group of students who receive specific, intensive training in mediation. There are several models of mediation, but all tend to follow the same general process in which mediators (a) provide a supportive environment in which disputants tell their versions of the problem, (b) focus disputants on mutually identified problems, (c) help disputants develop a list of possible solutions through brainstorming, and (d) guide disputants to mutually agreed upon resolutions. The negotiation skills required for mediators and disputants include self-control, effective communication, problem solving, critical thinking, and appropriate planning.

Providing students with the opportunity to develop negotiation skills should help to improve their self-esteem and contribute to a school climate that fosters peaceful solutions to interpersonal problems. After students have had positive experiences in settling their own disputes, they are better able to accept structure and guidance and are more self-motivated. The experiences gained through peer mediation can thus increase how much students benefit from traditional classroom settings. Other positive outcomes may include (a) a regard for conflict as a learning opportunity, (b) a nonpunitive method of discipline that has long-lasting benefits, (c) a reduction in violence, vandalism, and absenteeism, and (d) a better understanding of individual differences.

Conflict Resolution in Middle School

We can view the prevention of chronic behavior problems through conflict resolution strategies within a developmental frame of reference. Although younger children can learn to use conflict resolution strategies, we think these techniques are particularly relevant during the middle school years. In middle school, children are becoming increasingly independent of adults and more influenced by their peers. Programs that are appealing and instructive help students effectively meet the challenges encountered during this critical transition from childhood to adolescence.

Students who develop positive coping strategies for the environmental demands they encounter have an improved chance of growing into emotionally healthy adults. Such development requires that students learn new ways of conceptualizing and dealing with situations when their prior responses no longer work. Developmental psychologists call this process of creating new cognitive structures *accommodation*. Accommodation takes place when a person's former developmental level is no longer adequate to meet new environmental demands, and it occurs most readily under conditions that provide optimal levels of both *challenge* and *support*. Sufficient challenge is required to create a need to develop new ways of solving problems. Sufficient support is needed to create a climate in which the individual feels safe enough to risk trying new coping strategies. Successful development occurs when a challenge is balanced with available support.

A significant source of challenge for middle school students is conflict with their peers. Peer conflicts are troublesome for students who experience them and can significantly affect the entire school, the families involved, and the community. Peer mediation can offer a support system for some of the social challenges students experience and contribute to a developmentally appropriate environment within the school setting. The primary developmental tasks of adolescents are (a) achieving emotional independence from parents and other adults, (b) desiring and achieving socially responsible behavior, and (c) acquiring a set of values and an ethical system to guide behavior. Conflict resolution principles practiced through peer mediation can contribute to students' successful social adjustment and self-enhancement. . . .

A Model Program

Over a 4-year period, we collaborated with school personnel in three middle schools in the Southeast to establish and evaluate a conflict resolution program that included peer mediation. The school populations ranged from 780 to 1,135 students and were ethnically and socioeconomically diverse. From 32% to 61% of the students received a free or reduced-price lunch, and from 12% to 16% were designated as having a disability. Our goals included introducing students and staff to the basic tenets of conflict resolution, establishing positive attitudes about conflict within the school community, and reducing student office referrals for interpersonal conflict.

The task in teaching effective conflict resolution is to help students realize that their approach to conflict, rather than the existence of conflict itself, determines their successful social development. Our main objective was to show students how to make dealing with conflict a productive exercise. We developed a curriculum to foster a problem-solving approach to conflict and to encourage students to seek mutually agreeable solutions. We designed twelve 40- to 50-minute lessons within four topic areas: understanding conflict, effective communication, understanding anger, and handling anger. An additional lesson provided an introduction to the process of peer mediation. Lessons included student activities and role plays for practicing newly learned skills. We provided teachers with all materials, including instructional directions and sample scripts, overhead transparencies, and student worksheets. For example, students learned about the "Relax-Breathe-Think" model to practice thinking through difficult situations, rather than reacting impulsively, in a lesson on handling anger. Teachers then presented students with several scenarios and instructed them to answer the question, "Who's the boss, me or the problem?" in each case.

Administrative personnel in each school determined how the CR lessons would be integrated into their overall programs. In one case, a newly instituted course in critical thinking for students at all three grade levels provided an appropriate vehicle. In another school, a homeroom period at the beginning of the day was long enough to allow teachers to deliver the curriculum schoolwide. We encouraged teachers to highlight the lessons throughout the school year, providing opportunities for students to recognize and handle their anger, think through cooperative solutions to conflict, and practice effective listening and communication skills.

The Peer Mediation Program

Along with teaching students about effective conflict resolution skills, we also helped school personnel establish a peer mediation program. We provided training, program parameters, and implementation strategies, but each school developed its own method for selecting mediators and establishing mediation protocols. In each case, however, 25 to 30 students representing all three middle school grade levels served to mediate disputes throughout the year.

The peer mediation (PM) training included concepts similar to those covered by the schoolwide curriculum, such as understanding the nature of conflict and effective communication. It also focused on issues such as cultural influences, confidentiality, skills related to effective communication, and the specific procedures of the mediation process. Training included role plays and mediation simulations. Those who successfully completed the training were able to execute the mediation process with minimal supervision or intervention by adults.

A systematic referral process provided schoolwide student access to peer mediation. Referral forms were available to students and staff (e.g., in classrooms or guidance office), providing a record of the referring party, conflict location, brief description of the problem, and disputant names. Most important, participation in the peer mediation process was always voluntary. At the conclusion of each mediation, mediators and disputants signed an agreement form that included the date, type of conflict, and agreed-upon resolution. Although a teacher or counselor was available during mediation in case adult intervention became necessary, the supervision they provided was minimal.

According to the teachers with whom we worked, students' feelings of independence in handling their own disputes positively influenced their attitude toward the program and their willingness to take their responsibilities seriously.

The more challenging aspects of a schoolwide program are assuring that mediations occur as soon as possible after a referral is made and providing ample opportunities for all trained mediators to mediate disputes. An additional challenge is matching mediators appropriately with disputants (e.g., age, gender). School personnel paired mediators to provide mutual support, more frequent mediation opportunities, and to facilitate discussion during debriefings. We found the availability of a class period during which program facilitators could schedule mediations and meet regularly with mediators to debrief (e.g., a homeroom period) to be a help, if not a necessity. It may be possible to devise a schedule for varying the periods during which mediations occur, but it is not always easy to find suitable locations and provide supervision. Academic considerations also were given appropriate priority to prevent mediators from missing a test or important class presentation, if possible.

To summarize, setting up the peer mediation programs required significant planning and school resources. Those in charge of its implementation had to address the following questions as they considered the logistics of referrals and the mediation process:

- How and by whom would students be referred?
- What kinds of conflicts are suitable for mediation?
- Where would mediation take place?
- Who would supervise the mediations?
- How would the mediators be made available?
- How often would mediators miss class?
- Could teachers refuse to release a mediator (or disputant) from class to attend a mediation?

As we assisted in the implementation of the conflict resolution and peer mediation program in three middle schools and collected mediation data, we examined the patterns of office referrals, conflict issues, and mediation resolutions. Our findings are specific to the populations in the three schools, yet they generally correspond to those of other researchers. They also provide insight into how students use peer mediation and whether they consider it a viable alternative to less constructive conflict resolution strategies.

Who Are the Disputants?

Younger middle-school students appear to be more open than their older peers to using mediation to settle disputes. Sixth-grade students were involved in the majority of referrals to mediation. Of course, more disputes that can be handled appropriately through mediation, such as conflicts over relationship issues or feelings, may occur among sixth graders than among seventh or eighth graders. A higher frequency of these issues among younger students would result in a disproportionate number of sixth-grade mediations. From a developmental standpoint, however, there is reason to believe that as students progress through middle school, their need for independence grows. This may include a need for independence from any kind of help in settling conflicts, including the help of peers. One mediator told us that some students would feel embarrassed if they went to mediation, because their friends would ask them where they went. These students thought they risked their reputation if their friends found out they requested help.

We also found that more girls than boys participated in mediation. Some of the peer mediators suggested that mediation may be inherently less appealing to boys because they may perceive its use as a sign of weakness. For example, one student interviewed stated that his male peers might not use mediation because they wanted to put up a "tough" front with their friends and thereby "boost their reputation." Some boys might avoid *any* process that implied a need for assistance or a reluctance to solve interpersonal conflicts through force. To have a positive effect on school climate, peer mediation has to be socially acceptable to as many students as possible and particularly to those inclined to use aggression.

What Are the Conflict Issues?

Verbal harassment such as name-calling, threatening, or insulting a family member was the reason for most of the mediations. Spreading a rumor or talking behind someone's back (i.e., gossiping) were other frequently named issues. We found mild forms of physical aggression, such as pushing or hitting, to be less prevalent. Boys were more likely to be involved in some form of physical aggression, and girls were more likely to be concerned with relationship issues, such as broken friendships or gossip.

The high occurrence of verbal harassment issues in mediation has important implications for the prevention of serious conflict. Aggression theorists assert that verbal taunting, name-calling, or threats can escalate into physical aggression. This is especially the case for students who are deficient in the verbal skills necessary to de-escalate potentially violent situations. For these students, peer mediation is an opportunity to resolve negative verbal incidents by practicing effective verbal strategies in a structured environment and avoid an escalating chain of destructive events. If mediation can diffuse the effects of minor verbal threats or incidents before they become serious, it will serve an important preventive function.

An interesting question is whether the tendency for girls to be less involved in physical incidents and more involved in verbal ones is related to their greater tendency to refer themselves to mediation. Perhaps a preference for verbal strategies in negotiating social relation-ships in general makes girls respond more positively to a process that depends upon the use of verbal skills. If so, it underscores the need for program coordinators to address the social acceptability of peer medi-ation for male students. Some researchers have suggested that there is a relationship between level of verbal skill and use of physical aggres-sion among preadolescents. The more verbally skilled a child is, the *less* likely he or she may be to use physical force in resolving conflicts. If so, it is important (a) to teach students to negotiate verbally and (b) to give them opportunities to practice the required skills. Properly implemented peer mediation programs provide a vehicle for enhanc-ing verbal skills during a critical developmental period.

What Are the Typical Student Resolutions?

First, we observed over several years that more than 95% of media-tions resulted in a resolution acceptable to both disputing parties. This finding supports the notion that middle school students can, at the very least, successfully follow a structured procedure and help dis-putants reach some mutually agreeable conflict solution. The quality of the solutions they reached is also of interest. In our study, students most frequently resolved to avoid each other, stop the offending behavior, or "agree to get along." These data support findings from other studies of peer mediation at the elementary or middle school level in which researchers looked at the type of resolution reached.

The quality of an agreement reached by students through peer mediation may result from a variety of factors. First, we found that the older the *peer mediators*, the more likely resolutions involved an agreement to "get along" rather than simply to avoid each other or stop the offending behavior. This implies a developmental progres-sion in ability to facilitate productive communication and/or to stick with the negotiation process until disputants reach a more socially constructive solution. Early into our work in conflict resolution, we did not consider avoiding each other or simply terminating verbal or physical aggression to be desirable resolutions that would serve to strengthen the relationship between the disputing parties. As we con-tinued our study, we realized that the willingness and ability of 11-and 12-year-old mediators and disputants to follow a process of nego-tiation through to any acceptable solution is a significant achieve-ment and may provide a foundation for lifelong negotiation skills.

What Are the Overall Program Effects?

We intended to measure the effect of a comprehensive conflict resolu-tion/peer mediation program on the rate of referrals for disciplinary incidents, and on the attitudes of various members of the school com-munity. We accomplished that by examining school discipline rec-ords and by administering teacher and student attitude surveys about school conflict and school climate. With one exception in more than 20 student or teacher subscales, including those in surveys given to peer mediators, we did not find any significant changes in survey responses following program implementation. We believe that competing school priorities, which resulted in a curriculum of only five lessons per academic year, diminished the program's overall effect on student attitudes and school culture. We did, however, find a promising downward trend in disciplinary incidents, particularly at the school where staff were most involved. At that school, the peer mediation program was started early in the fall semester each year, the responsibility for training and student support was clearly assigned, and a homeroom period for mediations was available every day. This classroom period also provided a time for mediators to debrief with teachers and discuss their experiences. We consider each of these factors important for effective program implementation, and they may have resulted from a strong commitment and ownership of the program on the part of school administration and faculty. Our findings suggest that these accommodations affected the program's impact on school discipline. Concurrently, the factors themselves may also have contributed to the level of program acceptance by making the required activities more feasible to carry out.

Despite little evidence of schoolwide attitude change, mediators and disputants expressed high levels of satisfaction with the mediation process and its capacity for solving conflicts. Peer mediators and their parents reported that mediation skills learned during training were used frequently when conflicts arose at school outside of formal mediation or at home. Disputants, who were surveyed at least a week following mediation, reported continued adherence to their mediation agreement and high satisfaction with the process.

Student Perceptions of Their Teachers

The only consistent attitudinal change we found was in how mediators rated their teachers' communication. Following training in mediation, students' ratings of teacher communication were significantly lower than before training, when compared to the ratings of a control group who had not received training in mediation. More specifically, after students learned about the importance of (a) effective listening and speaking, (b) being open to others' ideas even when they are opposed to one's own, and (c) giving others a chance to express their ideas, students apparently raised the standards they used to judge their teachers in these areas.

The change in student perceptions of teacher communication following student training is an important finding. Since a significant portion of the peer mediation training was about the development of effective communication, students trained in mediation skills evaluated their teachers more harshly than their untrained peers did. This finding underscores the importance of establishing a school culture that supports the principles of positive conflict resolution and mediation. If teachers do not model effective communication and negotiation skills, the long-term impact of a program that incorporates peer mediation to influence patterns of student communication and conflict management is likely to be compromised.

THE WHOLE SCHOOL APPROACH TO VIOLENCE PREVENTION

Joan N. Burstyn and Rebecca Stevens

In the following selection, Joan N. Burstyn and Rebecca Stevens argue that to be truly effective, programs to reduce school violence must involve all members of the school community, including students, parents, teachers, administrators, and school bus drivers. Similarly, the authors stress, conflict resolution skills and cooperative principles need to be emphasized throughout the entire school curriculum. According to Burstyn and Stevens, the whole school approach enables the school community to learn and practice conflict management together, reinforcing the values of inclusiveness, tolerance, and nonviolence. Burstyn is a professor of education at Syracuse University in New York and the principal investigator of the Syracuse University Violence Prevention Project. Stevens is a professor of education at the University of South Carolina in Spartanburg.

Televised pictures of students who have killed their school fellows with handguns; newspaper stories of a teacher disarming a student in the classroom; and telephoned bomb threats that close down schools for searching, while students shiver on sidewalks and in parking lots, watching; all these foster a belief that public schools are no longer safe. What has happened to cause these events? In 1993, John E. Richters of the National Institute of Mental Health wrote: "In a few short years the widespread availability and use of handguns has transformed childhood into something quite foreign to what most adults can recall of their own childhoods." By 1993, those who lived in the cities understood the effect of handguns on adolescents, especially those drawn into the traffic of illegal drugs. However, it was not until 1997–1998 that the nation at large became aware of just how far childhood, for all children, had been transformed by them. During those years, headline news on television and in newspapers across the country announced that, in a series of incidents, boys had shot to death several people at schools in Pearl, Mississippi, West Paducah,

Joan N. Burstyn and Rebecca Stevens, "Involving the Whole School in Violence Prevention," *Preventing Violence in Schools: A Challenge to American Democracy*, by Joan N. Burstyn et al. Mahwah, NJ: Lawrence Erlbaum, 2001. Copyright © 2001 by Lawrence Erlbaum Associates, Inc. All rights reserved. Reproduced by permission.

Kentucky, Jonesboro, Arkansas, and Springfield, Oregon. The killing did not stop in 1998. Similar incidents, some perpetrated by even younger boys, have occurred since then each year.

Yet, even after these high-profile killings and even in neighborhoods known for their violence, schools remain relatively safe places for children. They are safer, that is, than their homes and the streets. There, children are in danger of violence, not only from their peers, but from adults as well. Nevertheless, it is school violence that has persuaded parents and educators to intensify their efforts to teach all children how to handle disputes nonviolently. This is a national issue because violence threatens the democratic principles of our multicultural society. If we, the citizens of our country, cannot handle disputes non-violently, we will soon destroy the fabric of democracy in the United States.

Often administrators and teachers need immediate help with crisis situations; and those of us who offer education in violence prevention and conflict resolution do provide information on crisis management. However, our main work has to be with administrators and teachers and must focus on ways to prevent crises from arising in the first place, through a curriculum that builds civility by teaching tolerance for others unlike ourselves and skills such as anger management, active listening, the sophisticated use of language, negotiation, and mediation. These are skills that individuals need in order to sustain a democratic community.

The Whole School Approach

For more than a decade, many onetime or one-grade-level interventions have been offered in schools, as though by inoculating students we could provide them with protection against violence and teach them how to deal with conflict peacefully. Often these interventions have languished because they have been add-ons to the regular curriculum, given to no teacher's or administrator's protection and nurturance. [We propose] a plan for integrating violence prevention and conflict resolution education into the fabric of a school.

To do this, we have not only to offer add-on education in the skills already referred to; we must also help teachers draw inferences about ways to handle conflict from the material they teach every day, such as the stories they ask students to read and the history or the science they teach. We have to ask them to explain to their students how cooperative learning in the classroom is part of learning to work together in a community without resorting to violence, that conflict is a process that can be either creative or destructive, and that violence (either verbal, psychological, or physical) is the most destructive outcome of conflict. The classroom can become an important site where students can learn positive ways to handle conflict. Such education is needed now in all schools, whether or not they have experienced outbreaks of violence.

A whole school approach to violence prevention aims at changing people's beliefs, attitudes, and behaviors so that violence will be reduced. It calls for a commitment to change on the part of everyone associated with the school. In the city where our research was conducted, we worked not only with the schools, but also with the students' parents and other members of the community. We did so because we perceive that school, family, and community all have roles that impact on one another in shaping children's behaviors and attitudes. We have found the contextual systems model, formulated by R.C. Pianta and D.J. Walsh, to be a useful tool for understanding how the family-and-child, as one system, and the school, as another system, interact. We perceive, also, that within a school there are subsystems, each with its own set of rules and sphere of influence, that interact with each other.

Changing the Environment

Within the academic curriculum, a whole school approach to violence prevention commits teachers to teach, and students to learn, ways of handling conflict constructively at all grade levels. The whole school approach enables students to build their skills in this area from one grade to the next. It encourages teachers to incorporate knowledge about conflict resolution into all subjects and to establish democratic processes for resolving conflicts peaceably in their classrooms.

Beyond the classroom, a whole school approach to violence prevention involves all school personnel in developing new skills of communication. Ideally, people in all roles, such as schoolbus drivers, teachers, secretaries, and administrators, meet in heterogeneous groups to discuss ways to reduce conflicts and to refresh their communication skills through a greater understanding of cultural differences and knowledge of anger management, negotiation, and mediation. By doing so, they will be better equipped to reinforce positive behaviors among the students and, incidentally, also among themselves. Because it commits all those in a school to learning new ways to handle conflicts, a whole school approach to violence prevention has the potential to change the entire environment. All become involved with learning new forms of knowledge and new ways of behaving. Thus, a whole school approach, based on teaching civility through a democratic process, can transform the ecology of the school. . . .

Violence Prevention and the Classroom Environment

Creating a Safe Space. A democratic classroom is important for establishing a safe environment in which to practice violence prevention and conflict resolution. Judicious discipline is but one way to create such a space. Another may be found in the introduction to *Creative Conflict Resolution*, where William J. Kreidler, of Educators for Social

Responsibility, identified the main causes of classroom conflict. Kreidler placed each cause in one of six categories: competitive atmosphere, intolerant atmosphere, poor communication, inappropriate expression of emotion, and misuse of power by the teacher. Later, he devoted a whole chapter to "resolving student vs. teacher conflicts," in which he described the power games that teachers play, usually because "they confuse authority with authoritarianism." He then outlined ways to establish goals that are mutually satisfying for the students and the teacher, as well as ways to establish effective rules that "prescribe positive behavior and list a range of consequences for not behaving that way."

Creative Problem Solving. Among the techniques that can be practiced in a safe, democratic classroom is creative problem solving. Edward De Bono claimed that creative problem solving is an important component that is often left out of conflict resolution strategies. He advocated teaching adults and children, especially those of high school age, a variety of problem-solving skills, including what he called "lateral thinking." Lateral thinking calls for participants to interrupt the accepted way to proceed by suggesting new pathways, shortcuts, or alternative routes—solutions to a problem that overturn the accepted "givens." All ideas, including those considered far-fetched, are examined by a group calmly and without judgment. Those problem-solving skills would serve people, not only in interpersonal relations, but also in their academic work.

The use of creative problem solving for facilitating group activities has a long history in industry. For example, Synectics was introduced by G.M. Prince in the 1960s. It called for a cooperative structure for team meetings and new roles for team leaders as facilitators of creative problem solving. Prince's technique takes would-be problem solvers on a vacation from their task by asking them to develop an intricate series of analogies. After the analogies have led the problem solvers far afield, the facilitator guides them back to their task through a series of planned activities. Groups usually generate a greater array of solutions through this process than through conventional problem solving. In the 1970s, Synectics materials were adapted for various school subjects, such as social studies. The techniques suggested by Prince and De Bono can help students, both inside and outside the classroom, visualize new, and less confrontational, ways to interpret people's actions and motives.

There are, however, some inherent contradictions in traditional schooling that make experimentation with creative problem solving difficult. The first contradiction is that between teacher-centered education and student-centered education—between an emphasis on teaching and an emphasis on learning. At the root of this contradiction is the question: Who is to maintain control over what is learned and how it is learned? If the people designing a whole school approach decide to encourage students to think creatively, then teachers in the school may have to relinquish some of their control over the students' learning.

A second contradiction is between learning that is individual and individually assessed and learning through group interactions that is assessed by both the product of the group's activities and the process of collaboration among the group. How is such work to be graded? If teachers wish students to embrace group activities and function amicably while undertaking them, they may have to reconsider their grading system in order to reward group work appropriately.

Multicultural Education

Children and adults carry attitudes and beliefs from the wider society into the classroom. Ours is increasingly a multicultural society, where the conflicts we encounter often arise from differences of race and ethnicity. Such conflicts may result from differing cultural values and traditions. They may also arise, as may conflicts over gender, class, and disability, from differing amounts of access to power and influence. Christine E. Sleeter and Carl A. Grant mapped the different forms of power that accrue to students from their own cultural knowledge and classroom knowledge. Subsequently, they identified five approaches to multicultural education. Individuals designing violence prevention programs need to consider the outcomes they wish to achieve before adopting one of these approaches.

The *teaching the exceptional and the culturally different approach* is designed to build bridges between the students and the school. The strategy is to get those not already aligned with the school to fit into the system.

The *human relations approach*, based on the ideals of tolerance and acceptance, is realized through the promotion of positive feelings among all students. Differences are confronted on levels that are affective and relational, not cognitive or intellectual.

The *single group studies approach* to multicultural education targets a particular group to empower its members; to inform and educate them about the group's culture, including its history of victimization, and to lead members to understand the group's perspective. The orientation of this approach is to empower group members to act on their own behalf.

The *multicultural education approach* promotes equality and cultural pluralism. It focuses on both structural and personal issues. Structurally, its goal is to obtain power equity through institutional accessibility and equal opportunity. Personally, its goals are to use respect, understanding, and critical thinking to teach about differences.

The *education that is multicultural and social reconstructionist approach*, which is favored by Sleeter and Grant, differs from the multicultural education approach by its greater emphasis on preparing students to change the social structure in order to achieve equality. Differences are explored at political and institutional levels. By a social reconstructionist education, Sleeter and Grant mean one that envisions a society that empowers every group and individual within it to effect change.

Sleeter and Grant's typology of multicultural education spans issues that are relational and interpersonal to those that are structural and involve social justice. Thus, they offer a range of ways to think about differences among people and how they may be reconciled through education.

Violence Prevention and the Curriculum

How can preventing violence and learning how to resolve conflicts creatively become an integral part of the curriculum in schools? One answer would be to revolutionize the curriculum. Nel Noddings suggested that the curriculum we know should be replaced by one with caring at its center. Noddings suggested the following centers of care: self; inner circle; strangers and distant others; animals, plants, and the earth; the human-made world; and ideas. Educators may agree with Noddings that, ideally, teaching students to care is what schools should emphasize, especially public schools which protect the welfare of the community as well as the achievement of individuals. Nevertheless, many may doubt that such an emphasis will be adopted in their lifetime. So, short of a revolution in educational thought, what can be achieved? Noddings herself provided guidelines for introducing some components of her centers of care while retaining the curriculum as now structured. Those components could form part of a whole school violence prevention program.

As of now, many violence prevention programs are introduced as an add-on to the existing curriculum. Outside consultants provide one or two-day courses on conflict resolution strategies, anger reduction, or negotiation skills, sometimes for staff or students only, and sometimes for both. As add-ons, these courses tend to be marginalized. The curriculum in most schools is already full of requirements that cannot be laid aside. Teachers, therefore, may acknowledge the importance of violence prevention but be hard put to find time to teach it, unless gun violence has already taken place in their school or their district. . . .

Another way to address violence prevention is to incorporate it into the existing curriculum. This calls for more extensive teacher preparation than the add-on programs but is also more likely to ensure that teachers will incorporate violence prevention into their day-to-day work. This approach includes pedagogical methods, such as cooperative learning, that provide the opportunity for students to practice the micro skills needed for resolving conflicts, including turn taking, active listening, negotiating, and problem solving. Extensive practice of these skills is essential if individuals are to integrate them into their repertoire. Constructive controversy is another pedagogical process that builds on the skills developed in cooperative learning. In this approach to violence prevention and conflict resolution, students take turns developing the argument for each participant in a controversy. This provides them with the opportunity to understand their opponents' viewpoints in a non-threatening situation. Research suggests that children who learn the skills needed for the peaceful resolution of conflicts improve academically as well. . . .

Staff Development for Teachers

A whole school approach to violence prevention is far more advantageous to teachers than having their principal encourage them to adopt a program within their own classrooms. Let's assume the latter takes place. A teacher attends a districtwide in-service workshop for one afternoon or a series of afternoons. Then she or he returns to the classroom with notes taken during the workshops, photocopied handouts, and a manual of activities for use in class. Even if several teachers from the school attend the workshops, they will be unlikely to meet regularly afterwards to reflect on their practice of what was learned there. Essentially, each teacher returns to an isolated classroom with no support. Thus, the odds that any one teacher will continue thinking about the material, let alone place it at the forefront of classroom practice, are slim indeed.

A schoolwide program can address barriers that teachers face when trying to introduce a program in their own classroom. Three significant barriers are, first that teachers often feel incompetent to teach a program after a short immersion in it; second, they may receive no rewards from the principal for carrying it out; and third, the violence prevention program may get lost within the pile of innovations presented to teachers each school year. A whole school approach provides support for teachers who try out a program for the first time. The school schedule is adapted to provide teachers the time to meet and consider the implications of violence prevention education in the classroom and the curriculum. In some cases, school and university partnerships enable school personnel and university faculty to work together to design programs and assess their effectiveness. Such collaboration between schools and universities on violence prevention already exists in many places, and in some, as with an alternative school and the Syracuse University Violence Prevention Project, a version of a whole school approach is being instituted.

A successful schoolwide violence prevention program attends to both the school structure and the development of each teacher in terms of his or her learning. Teachers are encouraged to "examine their own beliefs and understandings, reexamine their premises about teaching and learning and modify their practice," according to V. Richardson and M.L. Hamilton. For the teachers, as for the students, "learning is an active process in which students construct and reconstruct concepts, premises, and theories," [Richardson and Hamilton write]. For the individual teacher, this process involves active participation with a group of colleagues.

The structure and organization of the school have a direct influence on the patterns of relationships among teachers. A. Hargreaves outlines four types of teacher relationships: *Individualism* is characterized by teachers who are isolated from others, within their own classrooms. *Balkanization* is characterized by teachers who associate with small groups of colleagues in similar situations, such as other math or fourth grade teachers. These individuals tend to identify with and remain loyal to their particular group. *Contrived collegiality* is characterized by procedures mandating particular joint projects. Finally, the *collaborative culture* is characterized by ongoing and continuous help, trust, and openness, which permeate all relationships among the staff. In such a culture, the staff is united. The development of a collaborative culture is the intention of a violence prevention program.

In a school with a collaborative culture, adults recognize that conflicts are bound to occur and that ways to discuss them openly and resolve them creatively need to be encouraged as part of the school's violence prevention. Adults are thus able to model the relationships they are encouraging children to develop.

Modeling Care and Collaboration

It seems likely that changes in beliefs, values, and attitudes in teaching parallel changes in the ways teachers relate to their colleagues; that is, in their characteristic patterns of association. Thus, as well as providing formal times for school personnel to discuss issues, a schoolwide violence prevention program has to provide opportunities for informal contacts. Research suggests that a significant amount of teacher learning takes place on an informal, day-to-day basis. These more casual interactions can be encouraged with a welcoming and comfortable faculty lounge, faculty lunches, and social events. It is important to give value to, and allow for, a relaxed "down time" when teachers can talk.

Administrators and teachers in the school have to provide examples of care and collaboration. Formal structures need to encourage cross-level working and study groups composed of professionals, semiprofessionals, and nonprofessionals, as well as peer observations and teacher research projects. These schoolwide structural changes may take time to introduce and maintain. They support individual teachers and other staff in developing and implementing violence prevention within their own classroom and practice.

Changing practice and beliefs is a dynamic activity that entails the scrutiny of both. Formal and informal staff development in the school encourages a spirit of inquiry to facilitate the examination of both practice and beliefs. "The inquiry orientation allows for an examination of personally held values, goals, and empirical beliefs as well as student learning and development," in the words of V. Richardson and P.L. Anders. Such an orientation allows for the infusion of new ideas and practices.

Two Forms of Resistance

However, a whole school approach to violence prevention sometimes meets resistance of two kinds: the first is to the ideals or content of violence prevention and conflict resolution education, and the second, to the need for collaboration entailed by a whole school approach to change. The first may occur because violence prevention and conflict resolution education, which includes cooperative learning, peace education, prosocial development, and social skills training, runs counter to the very lifestyles of many people in American society. Shifting from an individualistic, competitive, teacher-centered focus in schools may be threatening to some parents, teachers, and administrators.

The second form of resistance may be to the collaborative approach to change. This approach assumes that change will occur, not only for students and their curriculum, but also for teachers and administrators, both in their working relationships with one another and in their design and implementation of school policies.

Change is both difficult and exciting. Those who become involved in changing their beliefs and practices will have many questions and doubts. They also will acquire new perspectives and insights to share and test out. Teachers need to feel competent with a new program. Opportunities to discuss the changes they are implementing will enhance their level of competency and expertise concerning any new material. School change and staff development "is time consuming and requires dialogue in a trusting atmosphere," according to Richardson and Anders. Time for dialogue is particularly necessary when considering change on the organizational, relational, and individual levels. Individual teachers need complete support in order to bring a conflict resolution program successfully into their classrooms where children spend most of their time. . . .

A Vehicle for Change

We have outlined the means by which schools can make a significant change to positively affect the lives of their students. Schoolteachers and administrators often seek help to stop violence once it has erupted in their schools. In other cases, they want to prevent violence from occurring. However, violence prevention and conflict resolution education offers a vehicle for greater change than they usually envision. By instituting a whole school approach, teachers and administrators can effect a change in the overall ecology of the school.

For our pluralistic society to function civilly, each person needs to learn skills of relating positively to others, accepting differences, and finding creative ways to resolve conflicts. Each child enters school with some interpersonal skills. However, those skills need refining and expanding for the child to grow to adulthood with the ability to resolve conflicts creatively and without ever resorting to violence. We can guarantee that the majority of people will learn the skills needed to participate fully in our multicultural, democratic society only when we teach those skills in our public schools. A whole school approach to violence prevention provides the vehicle for doing that.

Preventing School Violence Aimed at Gay, Lesbian, Bisexual, and Transgender Youth

Mark Pope

Gay, lesbian, bisexual, and transgender (GLBT) students are frequently the target of violence in schools, Mark Pope observes in the following selection. However, he contends, violence against GLBT students can be prevented if school officials refuse to tolerate homophobia and create a culture of acceptance. Diversity training in school, says Pope, must include promoting respect for differences in sexual orientation as well as race and ethnicity. Teachers, administrators, and other school workers can model inclusiveness by supporting GLBT students and providing resources related to GLBT issues, he adds. Pope is a professor of counselor education, counseling psychology, and family therapy in the School of Education at the University of Missouri in St. Louis.

To prevent violence against GLBT [gay, lesbian, bisexual, and transgender] students, schools must take an active role in eliminating such harassment. In this [viewpoint], the role of parents and school workers is explored, along with specific issues dealing with separation (e.g., separate schools for GLBT youths) or culture change, deliberate psychological education, valuing differences, and the power of subtle signs.

The Role of Parents and School Workers

Parents and school workers often teach homophobic attitudes in subtle, and sometimes not so subtle, ways. Some adults do this quite consciously because they feel that this is the best way to negatively reinforce such behavior, that it will somehow persuade the child through their disapproval to not be gay or lesbian. For other adults, it is not a conscious process, only one that is ingrained and reinforced through others in their environment. They do not even think that they are emotionally victimizing the gay or lesbian child; however, when people the child trusts are joking about him or her, it is emotionally injuring.

Through persistent derogatory jokes, behavioral admonitions ("don't be a sissy" or "don't hold your hand that way, that's too gay" or "girls don't sit like that"), and overheard homophobic conversations, gay and lesbian children absorb these attitudes, becoming victims of the adults they trust and who profess love for them. How do these gay and lesbian children deal with this incongruity? [H.F. Besner and C.I. Spungin report:]

> Some respond by denying their sexual orientation and dating and engaging in sexual activities with members of the opposite sex, trying to pass as heterosexual. Others respond by developing a strong contempt for those gays and lesbians who are more open and obvious. They may take out their own sexual frustrations through varying degrees of aggression toward gay and lesbian members of the community. Other gay and lesbian teenagers respond by withdrawing from society and becoming shy and isolated. They are reluctant to join in social activities with friends and family and live in a world all their own. Some of these teenagers are so filled with self-hatred they cannot find anything acceptable or positive to say about themselves. Some seek out groups that believe their homosexual orientation can be changed. These individuals will go to great extremes and will be highly motivated to do whatever it takes to be straight.

In R.C. Savin-Williams's 1990 study predicting self-esteem among lesbian and gay youths, the teenagers with the highest levels of self-esteem felt accepted by their mothers, male and female friends, and their academic advisors. Lesbian youths who had positive parental relationships felt comfortable with their sexual orientation. Satisfying parental relationships, maternal knowledge of their homosexuality, and having relatively little contact with fathers predicted positive self-esteem for gay men. Mothers are important for self-esteem for both gay men and lesbians as they are viewed as considerably more supportive, warm, and compassionate than fathers. Early parent-child interactions, physical affection, childhood rearing practices, and family religious teachings are considered good predictors of the state of comfort with children's sexual orientation.

Messages that parents give to their children are important in the children's developing self-esteem. Phrases such as "Be who you are and never be afraid to express your feelings" or "I love you for you" or "It's okay to talk about anything with me, even if I do not like what you have to say, I will always love you" convey a message of unconditional positive acceptance no matter what the situation is. Unfortunately, parental words spoken in haste and anger can destroy years of positive communication. It is always important for parents to weigh the impact of their words before speaking them to their children. Never should a parent say to the child, "You are so stupid" or similar phrases even in joking, as these negative phrases are powerful and are rarely forgotten.

When a student comes out to school personnel, this is a major event in the student's life and deserves to be treated in a sensitive and caring way by the school worker. Some guidelines to help school personnel respond to students when they disclose their sexuality are posted at http://www.umsl.edu/~pope.

Separation or Culture Change

During the 1980s and 1990s, between the political far-right's attempts to take control of school boards and the unionization of school workers, the schools became the battleground on which was played many of the tough political questions of the day. During this time, the issue of what to do with GLBT students also came to the top of the school agenda.

Different schools had different responses. In the New York City schools, the Harvey Milk School was established in 1985 for gay and lesbian students who were not succeeding. In Dallas, Texas, a private school for lesbian and gay youths opened in 1997. In the Los Angeles Unified School District, Dr. Virginia Uribe established "Project 10," a dropout prevention program offering emotional support, information, and resources to young people who identify themselves as lesbian, gay, or bisexual or who want information about sexual orientation. The San Francisco Unified School District under the leadership of Kevin Gogan began a similar program called Project 21 shortly thereafter. Most other school districts have established programs like Project 10 and have not chosen to go with the separate school, which seems to isolate gay and lesbian students from the mainstream.

Changing the school culture is imperative in this process of stopping school violence against GLBT youths. Each school worker has a role in solving this problem, including administrators, teachers, counselors, and cafeteria, maintenance, and transportation workers. School workers need tools to combat this violence, which will enable them to at least promote an environment of tolerance or preferably to promote an environment of appreciating and valuing of the sexual minority youths. Just being a sympathetic teacher is not enough, as a self-report study found that over 62% of health and education professionals said they very much needed newer and more knowledge and skills to discuss and teach about homosexuality and bisexuality.

As reported in the February 10, 1999, issue of the *St. Louis Post-Dispatch:*

A school newspaper survey in the Kirkwood Call last year showed 61% of the students who had answered said they insult people every day using such words as "gay." [Kirkwood, Missouri High School Principal Franklin] McCallie equated his students' use of "gay" or "fag" as a putdown to a racial or ethnic slur. . . . In November, his teachers took a "Teaching Respect for All" workshop [created by the Gay, Lesbian, Straight Educators Network and Parents and Friends of Lesbians and Gays]. . . . "I just felt that it is so obvious that a principal and a staff of a high school ought to be on the side of safety for all students, that it really shouldn't be a monumental step whatsoever," he said. "I'm not telling you that everyone agrees on the subject of homosexuality. I think that we are in agreement that everyone be safe in the schools."

The "Teaching Respect for All" workshop was created by the Gay, Lesbian, Straight Educators Network (GLSEN) and Parents and Friends of Lesbians and Gays (PFLAG) and is an important resource in combating the violence against GLBT students and changing the school culture that tolerates such violence. As Principal McCallie said in the newspaper article, "You do not have to accept homosexuality as equal to heterosexuality, but you do have to accept that everyone should be safe in the schools."

Deliberate Psychoaffective Education

What connects the recent shootings in the schools with antigay violence is reported in the May 3, 1999, article and cover story in *U.S. News & World Report:* "Surely it is a rare and complicated convergence of factors. Still, experts see some common threads in the spate of shootings: These adolescent boys can't manage their emotions. They feel rejected, enraged, jealous." They were boys who never learned how to identify, accept, and cope with their feelings.

Boys are not taught how to handle feelings, not by their fathers or by the schools. . . . Elementary and secondary schools in the United States do an acceptable job of cognitive education, excellent on information, and okay on critical thinking, but most schools get an "F" when it comes to "affective" education. This is not what is being termed "moral education" or "character education"; it is *affective education, psychological education*, or *psychoaffective education*. Teaching these important affective skills, such as interpersonal, social, and psychological skills, is rarely included in any school curriculum even though such pioneers as N.A. Sprinthall have written about "deliberate psychological education" for many years.

The deliberate psychoaffective education of American children must become a priority or we will continue to see even more school killings by young people who feel they have no hope, no place to turn, no one to talk with, no one who listens, and no perspective on life. These youths feel that any little personal rejection or emotional hurt they have is a tragedy from which they can "never" recover. Only in touch with feelings of hurt and emotional pain and having no other interpersonal skills to cope with these overwhelming feelings, they blast away, killing some whom they feel have caused them that pain and many times innocent bystanders, but it is directed at the institution they know best. Their parents take their rage to their workplace as that is their primary institutional focus; their children take their rage to their schools.

For example, in the Jonesboro, Arkansas, massacre of 10 students and a teacher by an 11-year-old boy and a 13-year-old boy with semi-automatic weapons, shooting their victims as they exited school during a fire alarm, many of their classmates now tell how the boys had talked about doing this for a while. What caused this? According to news reports, one of the boys was "enraged" over having been "dumped by his girlfriend.". . .

Many people and the U.S. school systems undervalue psychoaffective education. Although the schools cannot cure all the ills of society, education is more than information and even more than critical thinking. It is also about who we are and who we love during a time in our lives (school age) when we have many questions about those issues. Not enough attention to these issues is given in the schools. Schools must educate the whole child, not just the cognitive part. What we are seeing is the effect of that omission.

School counselors are important to the total care and education of students, from elementary school through high school. The following three types of school counselor activities are examples of deliberate psychoaffective education in the school: school counselors providing mental health counseling, providing career counseling, and providing a safe place to openly discuss sex. The more homosexuality is treated as a taboo subject and not discussed openly, the greater the risk of homophobia and misinformation, and the greater the risk of violence to GLBT youths.

Valuing Differences

Respecting, appreciating, and valuing differences are essential to stopping the violence against GLBT students. [Besner and Spungin state:]

> Teachers, counselors, administrators, and parents need to be more outspoken in their desire to teach their children about developing positive self-esteem and greater acceptance of differences. Although most individuals would agree with this on a case-by-case basis, everyone seems to have his or her area of difficulty in the acceptance of diversity.

Because of this difficulty, inclusive diversity training workshops have been developed. *Inclusive* is used here to mean that "diversity" is inclusive of ethnic and racial minorities as well as sexual minorities.

An excellent tool in teaching individuals to appreciate and value human differences is the Myers-Briggs Type Indicator (MBTI), a Jungian personality inventory. One of the most important outcomes of using the MBTI is to teach the importance of the individual's opposite personality traits. For example, although one's personality preference may be for extraversion whereas others' may be for introversion, there is no inherent hierarchy in which one is better than the other; in fact, both are required for successful functioning in the world.

Other tools are available for teaching multicultural and diversity lessons, including GLSEN's "Teaching Respect for All" and Besner and Spungin's model workshop for educators on homophobia. The National Coalition Building Institute, B'nai B'rith, and the American Friends Service Committee all offer excellent workshops on these topics and more.

In terms of the school curriculum, it is important to integrate and infuse gay and lesbian examples into all courses when appropriate. For example, when discussing U.S. history and the role of Native Americans, it would be appropriate to mention the revered position of "winktes" and "berdaches" (Native American terms for GLBT persons) in the spiritual life of American Indians as the shaman or medicine person of the tribe as well as the many examples of female warriors. After reading "The Picnic," a story by African American author James Baldwin, teachers can discuss Baldwin's gay orientation and the results of having a double oppression (being gay and African American).

Finally, school workers who are themselves GLBT should be encouraged to disclose their sexual orientation and be offered support and employment protection. One openly gay or lesbian teacher can affect the atmosphere of the entire school in a positive way. The importance of GLBT role models cannot be overstressed, and openly GLBT school workers challenge the myths and stereotypes for all students, not just the GLBT ones.

The Power of Subtle Signs

There are also many ways of letting GLBT and questioning students know that you, as a counselor, teacher, administrator, or other school worker, are supportive of their struggle. If, because of the school district, you are unable to be as overtly supportive as you would like to be, there remain some other ways in which you can still relay the message of your support for GLBT students.

Here are a few of the more obvious ones:

1. Have a "safe zone" sticker at the entrance to your office or classroom (available from the Bridges Project of the National Youth Advocacy Coalition).
2. Stock your school guidance office and library with literature on gay and lesbian concerns (see http://www.umsl.edu/~pope).
3. Post on-line resources for GLBT students, such as International

Lesbian and Gay Youth Association (http://www.ilgya.org); Parents and Friends of Lesbians and Gays (http://www.pflag); Gay, Lesbian, and Straight Educators Network (http://www.glsen.org); Gay and Lesbian Teen Pen Pals (http://www.chanton.com/gay-teens.html); National Resources for GLBT Youth (http://www.yale.edu/glb/youth.html); Oasis (teen magazine) (http://www.oasismag.com); Outright (http://www.outright.com); Out Proud, National Coalition for GLBT Youth (http://www.cyberspaces.com/outproud); The Cool Page for Queer Teens (http://www.pe.net/~bidstrup/cool.html); and National Gay and Lesbian Task Force (http://www.ngltf.org).

4. Offer free family counseling services on campus to deal with the issues of homosexuality.
5. Use gay and lesbian positive examples in your teaching or counseling.
6. Use inclusive, stigma-free language in the classroom and in all communication, such as "partners" instead of "husbands and wives."
7. Post pictures of famous GLBT people (see http://www.umsl.edu/~pope).

By demonstrating an accepting attitude, school workers can send a strong message to students and create a tolerant environment within the entire school. The issues of tolerance, acceptance, and value can be explored under the umbrella of diversity.

The Big Picture

The relationship is clear between derogatory language directed against GLBT students by their peers and adults in the school setting and self-harmful behavior, such as attempted suicide, suicidal ideation, running away, bad grades, and truancy.

Furthermore, GLBT students are more likely to come out to their counselors than any other school worker, according to a survey of 262 men and women who were lesbian, gay, or bisexual. Friends were rated first, counselors second, teachers third, and principals last. Counselors must be prepared to deal with GLBT youths when they do present themselves for counseling.

Indeed changes are occurring for gay teens. On January 21, 1999, *CBS This Morning* reported a story titled "Gay Teen Teaches Tolerance," about Sam Hanser, a 16-year-old high school student in Newtown, Massachusetts. Hanser told of assaults at the hands of his classmates: "A lot of people called me faggot and spat on me and did a lot of annoying things," said Hanser. But as Massachusetts was the first state to pass a law making harassment of lesbian and gay students a crime, Sam has been empowered and taken on a role of leadership. He runs a hotline for lesbian, gay, bisexual, transgender, and questioning youths, and speaks publicly about GLBT youth issues. He closed by saying, "I think that seeing diversity starts the whole process of being comfortable and acceptance of different people."

In 1998, a jury in Louisville, Kentucky, awarded $220,000 to a 17-year-old girl because the school she attended acted with "deliberate indifference" by permitting other students to call her "lezzie," assault her, and attempt to rape her. In 1996, a Wisconsin high school student was awarded $900,000 in punitive damages from a school district because it did not adequately protect him from antigay harassment. Other lawsuits are working their ways through the courts, including the 12-year-old boy who is suing his Pacifica, California, school district for refusing to intervene in his years of harassment, and the gay teen who was brutally attacked by eight other students who secured the American Civil Liberties Union to aid his lawsuit against the Kent, Washington, school district.

A national organization called the Gay, Lesbian, and Straight Educators Network rated 42 of the nation's largest public school districts on their policies and programs designed to serve GLBT students and school workers. Only 4 districts got an "A": Los Angeles, San Diego, Philadelphia, and Dade County, Florida. Twenty major school districts received a grade of "D." According to spokesperson Kate Frankfurt, "that means nearly 2 million students go to school in districts that fail" in basic gay human rights.

A Change in Attitudes

Clearly the momentum is turning toward the protection of GLBT teens in schools. In 1993, Massachusetts became the first state to ban antigay discrimination in its schools and create a statewide "safe schools" program. The U.S. Department of Education issued guidelines in March 1997 spelling out that gay teens are covered by federal prohibitions against sexual harassment.

Attitudes on sexuality are indeed changing, and this should bode well for gay teens, and ultimately the entire GLBT community. Although the message is not as strong as many of us would like, it is becoming clear that people can have their own private hatreds; however, when this becomes public as physical or verbal harassment or written into policy, it will not be allowed. The harassment of sexual minority students and teachers should not be tolerated.

Heterosexism, which according to Audre Lorde is defined as a "belief in the inherent superiority of one pattern of loving and thereby its right to dominance," and homophobia, which is the fear of being gay and hatred of gays and lesbians, must be exposed just as racism and sexism have been.

The Massachusetts Governor's Commission on Lesbian and Gay Youth issued a report in 1993 that summarized succinctly a blueprint for ending violence in the schools against gay and lesbian youths. The recommendations included the following:

1. School policies that protect gay and lesbian students by (a) antidiscrimination policies that include sexual orientation for students and teachers, including teacher contracts; (b) policies that guarantee equal access to education and school activities; (c) antiharassment policies and guidelines that deal with handling incidents of antigay language, harassment, or violence; and (d) multicultural and diversity policies.
2. Training teachers in suicide prevention and violence prevention as well as changing teacher certification requirements and school accreditation to include this training.
3. School-based support groups for gay and straight students.
4. Curriculum that includes gay and lesbian issues.
5. Information in school libraries for gay and lesbian adolescents.

As a consequence of this report, the Massachusetts Board of Education unanimously adopted the nation's first state educational policy prohibiting discrimination against lesbian and gay elementary and secondary school students and teachers. Many cities in the United States have adopted similar policies in their schools.

The lives of GLBT students in the schools are getting better, and the sad picture painted by many may not apply to all GLBT youths. However, it is important not to minimize the detrimental effects of verbal and physical violence and harassment on GLBT students' academic performance and social development. What counselors, teachers, administrators, and other school workers must focus on are the recommendations in this [viewpoint] for improving the school environment and the quality of life for GLBT students. It just makes it better for all students.

Helping Children Who Have Violent Tendencies

Anne G. Garrett

In the following selection, Anne G. Garrett emphasizes the importance of identifying children with violent tendencies as early as possible so that they can receive the help they need. Children at risk for violent behavior can benefit from effective intervention programs, Garrett asserts, which have been proven to reduce aggression and antisocial behavior. She provides an overview of several different types of primary and secondary intervention programs that address the special needs of at-risk children and teenagers. The key to reducing school violence, she argues, is to empower young people and the adults who serve them with effective conflict management skills. A public school educator for more than twenty years, Garrett is the associate superintendent of curriculum and instruction for Haywood County Schools in North Carolina.

A checklist developed from . . . characteristics of children with violent tendencies includes:
1. Has a history of tantrums and uncontrollable angry outbursts.
2. Characteristically resorts to name calling, cursing or abusive language.
3. Habitually makes violent threats when angry.
4. Has previously brought a weapon to school.
5. Has a background of serious disciplinary problems at school and in the community.
6. Has a background of drug, alcohol or other substance abuse or dependency.
7. Is on the fringe of their peer group with no close friends.
8. Is preoccupied with weapons, explosives or other incendiary devices.
9. Has previously been truant, suspended or expelled from school.
10. Displays cruelty to animals.

11. Has little or no supervision and support from parents or a caring adult.
12. Has witnessed or been a victim of abuse or neglect in the home.
13. Has been bullied or bullies peers or younger children.
14. Tends to blame others for difficulties and problems.
15. Consistently prefers television shows, movies or music that express violent themes.
16. Prefers reading materials that reflect violent themes, rituals and abuse.
17. Reflects anger, frustration and the dark side of life in school essays, doodlings or drawings.
18. Is involved with a gang or cult.
19. Has been cruel to animals.
20. Is fascinated with fire and fire setting.

Each item on the checklist is valued at five points. Five to 20 points—Indicates potential violence. Twenty-five to 50 points—Child is definitely at risk and immediate intervention needs to take place. Fifty-five to 100 points—Child and his family are in immediate danger of harm being inflicted on children or family. A request needs to be made to social services and law enforcement. Professional help is required.

Effective Intervention

The urge to prevent further school shootings and violence has led to a proliferation of antiviolence interventions for children, youth and their families. Those programs that have been evaluated and show promise include interventions aimed at reducing risk factors or at strengthening families and children to help them resist the effects of detrimental life circumstances.

Effective intervention programs share two primary characteristics: (a) they draw on the understanding of developmental and sociocultural risk factors of antisocial behavior; and (b) they use theory-based intervention strategies with known efficacy in changing behavior, tested program designs, and validated, objective measurement techniques to assess outcomes. Other key criteria that describe the most promising intervention approaches include the following:

- They begin as early as possible. Evidence indicates that intervention early in childhood can reduce aggression and antisocial behavior.
- They address aggression as part of a constellation of antisocial behaviors in the child or youth. Aggression is the number one problem behavior found in the aggressive child. Often the cluster includes academic difficulties, poor interpersonal relationships, cognitive deficiencies, and attribution biases.
- They include multiple components that reinforce each other across the child's everyday social contexts: family, school, peer groups, media and community. Aggressive tendencies are displayed within the different components.

- They take advantage of developmental windows of opportunities: points at which interventions are especially needed or likely to make a difference. Windows should include transitions in a child's life: birth, entry into preschool, the beginning of elementary or middle school, and adolescence. The developmental challenges of adolescence are a particular window of opportunity, because the limits-testing and other age-appropriate behaviors of adolescents tend to challenge even a functional family's well-developed patterns of interaction.

Primary Prevention Programs

Prevention directed early in life can reduce factors that increase risk for antisocial behavior and clinical dysfunction in childhood and adolescence. Among the most promising interventions are:

Home visitor programs for at-risk families, which include prenatal and postnatal counseling and continued contact with the family and child in the first few years of life. In a 20-year follow-up of one such program positive results could be seen both for the child and mother.

Preschool programs that address diverse intellectual, emotional, and social needs and the development of cognition and decision-making processes. Two good examples of these programs include Smart Start and Title I Pre-Kindergarten. Smart Start is supported greatly by Governor Michael Easley in North Carolina and focuses entirely on the parenting and home aspects. Title I has an excellent parent component in which parents are required to participate if their children are eligible. For the Title I classes 16 children are selected who are educationally deprived.

School-based primary prevention programs for children and adolescents are effective with children and youth that are not seriously violence-prone, but these programs have not yet been demonstrated to have major effects on seriously and persistently aggressive behavior. Evaluations on such school-based programs show they can improve prosocial competence and reduce at-risk behavior among youth who are not seriously violence-prone by promoting nonviolent norms, lessening the opportunity for and elicitation of violent acts, and preventing the sporadic aggressiveness that engages temporarily during adolescence. The program teaches youth how to cope better with the transitional crisis of adolescence and offers them alternatives and institutional constraints to keep sporadic aggressiveness within socially defined bounds. Examples of these programs include teaching about adolescence, which is typically done in fifth and sixth grades and normally occurs during health classes. The focus is on body changes and the social and emotional aspects of the changes. Other programs might be Project Pursuit or Soaring High. Both of these programs focus on team building skills, trust and socially accepted behaviors.

Secondary prevention programs that focus on improving individual affective, cognitive, and behavior skills or on modifying the learning conditions for aggression offer promise of interrupting the path toward violence for high-risk or predelinquent youth. To the extent that development is an ongoing process, programs that target learning contexts, such as the family, should produce the most long-term effects. However, programs for youth that deal with aggressive behaviors have not been successful when they have been unfocused and not based on sound theory. Furthermore, because most programs have been relatively brief and have emphasized psychoeducational interventions, it is not known whether they would be effective with seriously aggressive or delinquent youth.

Programs that attempt to work with and modify the family system of a high-risk child have great potential to prevent the development of aggressive and violent behavior. Family variables are very important in the development and treatment of antisocial and violent behavior. For example, adolescents referred to juvenile court for minor infractions received an intervention with a family-therapy approach to identify maladaptive family interaction patterns; instruction for remedial family management skills was successful in reducing violence rates for up to 18 months. The counseling sessions dealt with parenting skills, setting parameters and getting assistance from professionals when it was necessary.

According to a report released by the Senate Judiciary Committee, the United States is now considered to be the most violent and self-destructive nation in the industrialized world. Domestic violence, assault, homicide, child abuse and neglect have become common characteristics of American life.

Conflict Management Skills

School crime and violence can be viewed as the tangible expression of unresolved conflict. If we empower young people and the adults who serve them with more effective conflict management skills, a more productive learning climate will result. When young people develop and apply nonviolent problem-solving skills, campus life can be dramatically improved.

When teachers and administrators train students in nonviolent problem-solving techniques, the working atmosphere among members of staff is often enhanced as a program by-product. When youth-serving agencies utilize these same skills and practices, a spirit of community cooperation and goodwill can emerge. Good conflict resolution skills, like violence, are contagious.

Infusing conflict management training into the curriculum offers hope to students and staff alike. Conflict management programs help children develop better behavioral skills, minimizing their opportunities for trouble and maximizing their opportunities for positive social interaction.

By intervening early, we stand a much better chance of providing young people with positive educational experiences that can provide the foundation for ongoing success. Educators no longer have a choice as to whether or not schools should be made safer and better for young people. It is imperative that we do everything in our power to create a climate that supports the safety, success and development of all children.

MEASURES TO PREVENT THE REJECTION OF STUDENTS BY THEIR PEERS

Karen F. Osterman

As Karen F. Osterman explains in the following article, one of the most isolating experiences that students can have is to be rejected by their peers. This type of rejection is often devastating to students' emotional health, Osterman warns, creating the extreme disaffection that can lead to school violence. Therefore, the author contends, fostering friendship in the school environment is crucial to reducing student violence. She recommends proactive steps for teachers and administrators that include enforcing ground rules against harassment and abuse, promoting a culture of tolerance and acceptance, and reaching out to students who are labeled as different. School activities designed to help students get to know each other better can go a long way in preventing unnecessary conflicts that result from rejection, she asserts. Osterman is an education professor at Hofstra University in Hempstead, New York.

I am both a parent and a professor. A few years ago, after hearing repeated complaints from high school students about how isolated and lonely they felt, I did a small observational study. Two doctoral assistants and I followed six students through an entire day. What we found was that these students—from high-, average-, and low-ability groups—had very little, if any, contact with other students during the school day. There were few opportunities to interact with peers in classes and little interaction in the halls or in the cafeteria.

The Significance of Peer Relationships

Many of my professional colleagues didn't seem too concerned about this, so I decided to look into the research more deeply and see what I could learn about peer relationships. Were they important, and what kinds of factors influenced the quality of the relationships among students? What I learned in an analysis of over 150 research studies has, I believe, important implications for preventing student violence.

First, we found that peer relationships were important, but not for the reason that I thought. Originally, I had thought that positive peer relationships would have a direct effect on student learning. But what I found was that the quality of students' relationships with teachers had the most direct and significant effect on students' involvement in learning. Peer relationships, however, had a very significant impact on students' emotional health. Rejection by peers was devastating and particularly so for boys with a high need for affiliation. This gender difference is probably related to the facts that boys have fewer friends and that masculine stereotypes make it difficult for boys to express their need for friends and emotional support. Boys who want to be accepted by other boys can't afford to complain or to seek adult assistance in dealing with their problems.

The other important finding was that many children in elementary and secondary schools have no friends and are not part of any group. Not being a part of a group, however, is not as important as is rejection. It's okay not to be popular. But if you're ostracized from the group, that's when the trouble begins. This is likely to be more problematic in secondary school than in elementary school simply because of the school structure. For the most part students in elementary school remain together with a single group of peers and a single teacher, but even this "family-like" arrangement is no barrier to bullying and victimization. At the secondary level, departmentalization contributes even more to fragmentation, and there are fewer opportunities for students to develop positive relationships with others.

Research also tells us a lot about what happens in schools that contributes to peer rejection and also what can be done to prevent it. The most important fact here is that students who are rejected by their peers are also rejected by their teachers and by other adults in the school. Students who are rejected by the whole school community, in effect, are those who are different in some way: they don't dress well, they're not physically attractive, and they're not socially attractive. They may be bright, but they're not typical learners. They either have behavior problems or are withdrawn. The behavior problems get attention from teachers, but it's negative attention. Those students who are withdrawn are no more able to develop a positive relationship with teachers than with their peers. This lack of support from anyone exacerbates the sense of emotional isolation.

Students who are rejected by teachers and peers become more and more isolated. Teachers avoid them or criticize them, and peers refuse to work with them in class or on projects. Feeling rejected, these students avoid even trying to join in extracurricular activities. It's hard for adults to enter a room where they know no one. It's even harder for a teen to enter a room when he knows that people don't like him and, even worse, might subject him to the type of verbal abuse—including attacks on his sexual identity—that cuts to the quick.

How to Prevent Rejection

So what can educators do about this? Research also establishes one extremely important point: if you give people a chance to interact, they will get to know one another, and, even if they don't become friends, they'll become more tolerant. What does this mean for schools? I believe that these and other findings suggest a number of strategies.

1. Establish the ground rules: harassment and abuse in the classroom and in the school are not acceptable. Young people respond to adult rules, and adults in schools are frequently aware of student harassment. In fact, much of it takes place right in the classroom. Like so many other people in our society, educators assume that this harassment is a natural part of growing up, and they often ignore it or blame the child who is being harassed. Tolerating harassment sends a message that it's okay. The rules need to be clear, and they need to be enforced.

2. Promote a culture of tolerance and acceptance. At a minimum, prevent abuse. But go beyond that to develop a culture that encourages not just tolerance for diversity, but caring and respect. This must be done through word and action. Express your values and encourage adults and students to extend themselves for others. Do unto others what you would have them do unto one another. Emphasize modeling and recognition, rather than control and punishment.

3. Reach out to students who are a little different. Students need adult support, whether they are in sixth grade or ninth grade. Sometimes it's difficult to approach young people, particularly teens, because their body language and even their spoken words convey a message to leave them alone. They don't mean it. Another important research finding is that people—youngsters and adults—need to feel that they belong and that the people they work with care for them. Adults can't tolerate working in a hostile environment; young people are even less prepared to do so.

Helping Children Blossom

Sometimes educators get so focused on academic learning that they forget that children have emotional needs. Students need to feel that others care about them, they need to feel that they are competent, and they need to have their autonomy respected. In an action research project designed to remedy the problem of bullying and victimization in elementary classrooms, a group of teachers working with their principal began by examining their own classroom practice. After observing for several weeks, they were surprised to find few occasions when the students were positively involved with the teacher or with peers and few opportunities for students to feel good about themselves.

With this new awareness, they began to interact more with victimized students. They talked to them about classwork and about their lives. They worked with them and figured out how to use their talents in the classroom. As a result, they found that they developed a new appreciation for these children. They liked them more, and they saw sides of their personalities that they had never seen. The children blossomed: they smiled more, they had more self-confidence, they became more engaged in classroom work, and they began to reach out more to the teacher and to their peers. Everyone responded.

Initially, the teachers expressed the opinion that the children—or their parents—were responsible for the way others treated them. This experience led them to change their thinking. They came to realize that they, as teachers, played an important role in shaping these students' experience in the classroom. They also realized that the quality of their interaction with these students seemed to affect how the other students treated the "victim." When they began to treat these students differently and demonstrated their affection and concern for them, the other students in the class did so too.

Children who are rejected are children who are neglected. Their behavior is a natural response to this rejection. Adults feel depressed when their colleagues don't like them. It's much worse for children, whose whole world is their school and friends.

Creating a Sense of Community

4. Provide opportunities for students to get to know one another. Most adults, educators included, assume that because teens tend to look alike and act alike, they're all part of one big happy group. That's a myth. Many students are isolated and have no chance in their classes to get to know one another. In the action research project I mentioned above, the teachers observed that cooperative learning groups would refuse to allow certain students to work with them. The teachers established rules that no one could be turned away. And the students who had once shunned some of their peers had experiences similar to those of the teachers: when they had a chance to work with these formerly rejected youngsters, they got to like them better. And students don't bully their friends. We need to help students to become friends.

Educators who work with adults regularly incorporate activities into the classroom that are designed to develop a strong sense of community. They use "ice breakers" to make sure that people in the group get to know one another. They assign people to groups, and they rotate membership in the groups. They use information about learning patterns to develop groups to ensure that they have the resources to be successful. Orientation programs and extracurricular activities are also important, but the largest part of any student's day is spent in the classroom. These strategies can also help younger students get to know and appreciate one another. The students' learning—and their emotional health—depends on it.

Implementing these strategies is not as simple as installing a metal detector, and it requires the effort of everyone in the school community—teachers, librarians, secretaries, administrators, guidance counselors, lunchroom monitors, custodians, and bus drivers. We need to make schools places where students can feel safe emotionally. Making that happen will go a long way toward ensuring their physical safety as well.

STOPPING STUDENT FIGHTS:
AN ACTION PLAN FOR TEACHERS

Lynette Fields

One of the most unsettling situations a teacher can face is a physical fight between students. In the following selection, Lynette Fields writes that the prevalence of school fights necessitates that teachers learn effective ways to respond. She recommends that teachers first become familiar with policies concerning student discipline in their states, school districts, and individual schools. After defining their duties and responsibilities, teachers need to receive training in effective intervention techniques that will help them create action plans to deal with various violent situations. Fields is an instructor of educational leadership at the University of South Florida in St. Petersburg.

I recently asked the students in one of my graduate Educational Leadership courses—they are teachers who are preparing to become school or district administrators—"What do you think is the most difficult problem facing teachers and administrators today?" Many voiced concerns about student discipline and school safety. One teacher described a frightening experience that she had encountered. She was supervising the hallway of her middle school during class changes when two female students began fighting. The teacher froze, unsure what she should do. She was concerned for her own safety and for the safety of the girls who were fighting. Before she could make a decision, a school resource officer in the vicinity tried to intervene. The girls continued fighting, and the resource officer was thrown to the ground trying to break up the fight. The teacher said that she was unnerved by not knowing what she should do and was shocked by the intensity of the fight. Although she had had five years of teaching experience, she had never been trained what to do when students engage in physical fights. She confessed that she relied on others to handle things and really didn't want to be involved. Another student pointed out that it was everyone's responsibility to maintain safety on school grounds. This student felt that the teacher had been negligent in doing nothing. This led to a heated debate about the problem of student-to-student physical confrontations, and most of the teachers wanted to know the answer to the question "What should I do?"

In this article I suggest a three-step plan to help teachers and administrators know what to do during student fights. I will also detail the extent of the problem of student-to-student physical confrontations.

Student-to-Student Physical Confrontations

The problem of student-to-student physical confrontations is quite serious. Principals, teachers, students, and the general public have voiced their concerns in several recent surveys.

The National Center for Educational Statistics surveyed principals and school disciplinarians in public elementary and secondary schools nationwide to obtain current data on school discipline problems. Student tardiness (40 percent), student absenteeism (25 percent), and physical conflicts among students (21 percent) were the top three discipline issues on the minds of the public school principals in 1997.

In a 1993 [L. Harris and Associates] survey of teachers, the major problems for teachers were students who were involved in pushing, shoving, grabbing, or slapping (28 percent). Students who verbally insulted others (26 percent) or stole (19 percent) were other major concerns.

A 2001 [Josephson Institute of Ethics] survey of U.S. teens (15,877 middle and high school students) reported that more than one in three students (39 percent of middle schoolers and 36 percent of high schoolers) said that they do not feel safe in schools. Thirty-seven percent of middle school boys and 43 percent of high school boys believed that it was appropriate to hit or threaten a person who makes them angry. Nineteen percent of the girls felt the same. Most alarming was that 75 percent of all boys and 60 percent of all girls said that they had hit someone in the past twelve months because they were angry.

In a 1998 Gallup Poll, citizens were asked what they thought were the biggest problems for public schools and communities, and the number one answer was fighting/violence/gangs (15 percent). The second most common response was lack of discipline (14 percent). Thus, one can conclude that physical confrontations between students occur frequently in our public schools. How should teachers or administrators intervene? What are their legal rights and responsibilities? In the following paragraphs, I will describe a three-step plan to answer these questions.

Do the Homework

The first step in preparing for physical altercations between students is to become familiar with written guidelines concerning the authority of school personnel and student discipline. Look for guidance in state statutes, state board of education rules, school board rules and regulations, instructional and noninstructional contracts, district policies, and school policies. Analyze these documents to clearly define

1. What authority is given to me, in my specific role, in dealing with student discipline?
2. When I exercise the authority given to me, how am I protected civilly and criminally?
3. What are the professional conduct expectations that apply to me when I am dealing with student discipline?

Speak with individuals in the school district to further define duties and responsibilities and to obtain a practical view of their application. Principals, directors of employee relations, assistant superintendents, superintendents, or union presidents are excellent resources. Determine the professional expectations and responsibilities of teachers and administrators in student discipline, specifically student fights. Commonly, the professional expectation includes providing protection or safety for students, but not at the expense of the protection or safety of the school employee. Although many school employees are fearful of touching students under any circumstances, most states and school districts allow physical intervention after attempts at verbal intervention have failed and when the student is in danger of harming him- or herself or others.

After completing research of state, district, and school policies and procedures regarding student discipline, a second major step is to receive instruction in verbal de-escalation, physical interventions, and physical restraints. Take advantage of inservice training that many school districts provide for school employees. There is one specific training course, "Non-violent Crisis Intervention," that covers both verbal and physical intervention. The course teaches several skills that maximize student safety and school employee protection. These skills include: how to verbally de-escalate situations; how to physically take down and restrain a student who has physically lost control; how to protect oneself if attacked by a student; and how to escape or assist others in escaping certain holds. It is critically important to know how to physically intervene without harming students or oneself.

Create a Mental Action Plan

To complete the preparation for dealing with student fights, use the knowledge gained from research and training to create a mental plan of action. The following is an effective general guideline proposed by Jim Davis, Director of Employee Relations of Pasco County, Florida, and Liz Geiger, President of United School Employees of Pasco County, Florida.

If a student fight occurs, to protect the safety of the students, school employees need to do the following:

1. Give a loud, clear verbal command.
2. Make a decision whether or not to physically intervene. Is it safe?

3. If it is not safe, decide how to get help quickly while adequately protecting the students in your care.

4. If it is safe, physically intervene. Use reasonable force and do not become the aggressor.

Let's review these guidelines using two examples. You are supervising a hallway in a high school. Suddenly two very large students begin fist fighting. First, give a loud, clear verbal command such as "Stop! Back away from each other and keep your hands to yourselves!" If you know the students' names, using them can be helpful in getting their attention.

If the students continue fighting, decide whether or not to physically intervene. Is it safe? There are many factors to consider. Some of these include the age of the students, their size, the intensity of the fight, the number of students involved, the use of weapons, and the presence of blood. Assume in this scenario that both students are larger than you and that the fight is at peak intensity. You have given a loud clear verbal command, and the students continue to fight. You have decided that, at this point, it is not safe for you to intervene physically. Now you must decide how to get help quickly while adequately protecting the other students in the hall. Depending on the circumstances, possible solutions at this point would be to

- ask adults who are close by for help;
- send a student to get other adults for help;
- use some form of communication such as an emergency call button on an intercom system, two-way radio, or telephone to get adult assistance;
- continue to give loud, clear verbal commands to the students who are fighting to stop;
- give loud, clear verbal commands to the students in the hall to keep away; and
- move objects out of the way that could cause harm such as desks, chairs, glass, and so forth.

When it becomes safe, physically intervene if necessary.

Student fights are stressful and emotionally draining experiences for teachers and administrators. Having full knowledge of your authority in such situations and being mentally prepared with a plan of action will provide the confidence and leadership necessary to deal with the affective side of this issue while protecting yourself and your students.

Consider a second example. Imagine you are supervising a hallway in a middle school. Suddenly two sixth grade students begin fighting. These students are half your size. First, you give a loud, clear verbal command. Second, you analyze the circumstances and decide that it is safe to intervene. Third, you intervene physically in such a way as to use reasonable force and to not become an aggressor. Again, inservice courses such as Non-violent Crisis Intervention Training will provide the training necessary to safely intervene.

THE PROBLEM WITH THE EXPANSION OF POLICE POWER IN SCHOOLS

Randall R. Beger

In response to the outbreak of high-profile school shootings, many school districts have increased the presence of law enforcement officials on school campuses. Randall R. Beger argues that this extensive expansion of police power is out of proportion to actual rates of school violence. In fact, he maintains, this trend has resulted in overly harsh punishments for relatively harmless student behavior. Beger is also concerned that recent court decisions have eroded civil liberties by exempting school environments from Fourth Amendment search-and-seizure protections. Students, the author counters, should be given the highest legal protection possible due to their subservient position in schools. Beger is a professor of sociology and the coordinator of the criminal justice program at the University of Wisconsin at Eau Claire. He has published numerous articles on juvenile justice and the legal rights of minors.

Growing public anxiety over acts of violence in schools has prompted educators and state lawmakers to adopt drastic measures to improve the safety of students. In the wake of recent high-profile campus shootings, schools have become almost prison-like in terms of security and in diminishing the rights of students. Ironically, a repressive approach to school safety may do more harm than good by creating an atmosphere of mistrust and alienation that causes students to misbehave.

This article examines law enforcement expansion in schools and the vanishing Fourth Amendment rights of public school children. The climate of fear generated by recent school shootings has spurred school administrators to increase security through physical means (locks, surveillance cameras, metal detectors) and to hire more police and security guards. State lawmakers have eagerly jumped on the school safety bandwagon by making it easier to punish school children as adults for a wide range of offenses that traditionally have been handled informally by teachers. Instead of safeguarding the rights of

Randall R. Beger, "Expansion of Police Power in Public Schools and the Vanishing Rights of Students," *Social Justice*, Spring/Summer 2002, pp. 119–30. Copyright © 2002 by Crime and Social Justice Associates. Reproduced by permission.

students against arbitrary police power, our nation's courts are granting police and school officials more authority to conduct searches of students. Tragically, little if any Fourth Amendment protection now exists to shield students from the raw exercise of police power in public schools.

The New School Security Culture and the Realities of School Violence

In response to the latest string of sensationalized school shootings, schools everywhere have made safety a top priority. A 1998 U.S. Department of Education survey of public schools found that 96% required guests to sign in before entering the school building, 80% had a closed campus policy that forbids students to leave campus for lunch, and 53% controlled access to their school buildings. A National School Board Association survey of over 700 school districts throughout the United States found that 39% of urban school districts use metal detectors, 75% use locker searches, and 65% use security personnel. Schools have introduced stricter dress codes, put up barbed-wire security fences, banned book bags and pagers, and have added "lock down drills" and "SWAT team" rehearsals to their safety programs. Officials in Dallas, Texas, unveiled a $41 million state-of-the-art "security conscious" school that has 37 surveillance cameras, six metal detectors, and a security command center for monitoring the building and grounds. At Tewksbury Memorial High School in Massachusetts, 20 video cameras bring the school into the local police department via remote access technology. According to one source, "the video cameras record almost everything students say and do at school—eating in the cafeteria, cramming in the library, chatting in the halls." The new security culture in public schools has stirred debate over whether schools have turned into "learning prisons" where the students unwittingly become "guinea pigs" to test the latest security devices.

Since the mid-1990s, a growing number of schools have adopted zero tolerance policies under which students receive predetermined penalties for any offense, no matter how minor. Students have been expelled or suspended from school for sharing aspirin, Midol, and Certs tablets, and for bringing nail clippers and scissors to class. There is no credible evidence that zero tolerance measures improve classroom management or the behavior of students. Such measures are not only ineffectual, but also appear to have a negative impact on children of color. Research indicates that black children are more likely than are whites to be expelled or suspended from school under zero tolerance.

Although most Americans believe that public schools are violent and dangerous places, numerous surveys on school safety contradict this notion. For example, according to U.S. Department of Education statistics, only 10% of public schools experienced one or more serious violent crimes during the 1996–1997 school year. Over the same period, almost half the nation's public schools (43%) reported no incidents of serious crime. Data from the Uniform Crime Reports show a decline of approximately 56% in juvenile homicide arrests between 1993 and 1998. In *Justice Blind? Ideals and Realities of American Criminal Justice*, Matthew Robinson explains why the conventional wisdom that schools are dangerous places is irrational:

> There are more than 51 million students and approximately 3 million teachers in American schools. In 1996, there were approximately 380,000 violent victimizations at school against these roughly 54 million people. This means the rate of violent victimization at U.S. schools is about 704 per 100,000 people. Stated differently, about 0.7% of people can expect to become victims of serious violent crimes at schools.

The odds of a child being killed at school by gunfire during the 1998–1999 school year were about one in two million. Contrary to media hyperbole about violence in public schools, most school-related injuries are nonviolent in nature, and the majority of crimes that occur in schools are thefts.

The Police Buildup in Public Schools

Despite the relative rarity of school violence, officials everywhere are feeling pressure to improve the safety of students and staff. An increasingly popular "quick fix" strategy is to hire police and security guards. According to a U.S. Department of Education study, about 19% of public schools had the full-time presence of a police officer or other law enforcement representative during the 1996–1997 school year.

School police officers take many forms. Some are regular uniformed police officers working on a part-time basis for a school district. Others are hired and trained by school security departments. In New York City alone, some 3,200 uniformed school security officers work in the Division of School Safety of the City Board of Education, "a contingent larger than the Boston Police Department," [according to researcher John Devine]. Many school districts use more than one form of police, such as campus police with support from local police or private security guards.

School Resource Officers (SROs) are the fastest-growing segment of law enforcement officials stationed in public schools. These armed and uniformed law enforcement officials perform multiple tasks, such as patrolling school grounds, assisting with investigations of students who break school rules, and arresting students who commit crimes. SROs also perform nontraditional law enforcement functions that include chaperoning dances, counseling students, and conducting seminars on substance abuse prevention. In 1997, there were 9,446 School Resource Officers in local police departments assigned to public schools in the United States. Their numbers have increased rapidly in recent years due to increased funding at the federal level to hire more officers. In the last two years alone, the Office of Community Oriented Policing Services (COPS) has awarded more than $350 million in grants to the COPS in Schools program to hire over 3,200 School Resource Officers at an annual cost of $54,687 each. Under a federal budget plan supported by President George W. Bush, COPS funding to hire school police will more than double.

Increased Police Power

The large influx of police officers in public schools has shifted the responsibility for maintaining order and discipline in the classroom away from teachers and into the hands of law enforcement officials. In *Maximum Security: The Culture of Violence in Inner-City Schools*, John Devine describes how school security police in New York public schools have "taken on an independent existence, with [their] own organization and procedures, language, rules, equipment, dressing rooms, uniforms, vans, and lines of authority." A school principal admitted to Devine: "I have no control over security guards, they don't report to me." Recently, the New York City Board of Education, at the urging of former Mayor Rudolph Giuliani, voted to transfer responsibility for school safety to the city police. School boards in other states, including California, Florida, and Nevada, have come out in favor of placing student safety under the control of city police.

The trend in support of moving school discipline in the direction of law enforcement has also been given a push by state lawmakers. In Arizona, for example, a new state law requires that school officials report any crimes or security threats involving students to the local police. Under a new Michigan statute, teachers must involve the police in any search of students' lockers, cars, and personal belongings. The law explicitly states that evidence obtained from a search by a police officer cannot be excluded in a court or school disciplinary hearing. States have also enacted legislation that requires school officials to share information about students with police, including personal information gathered by school therapists and counselors.

Concurrently, state lawmakers have dramatically increased the penalties for crimes committed on school property. In Mississippi, the penalty for having a gun on school property is a fine of up to $5,000 and up to three years in prison. Louisiana law prescribes that any student or nonstudent carrying a firearm on school grounds "shall be imprisoned at hard labor for not more than five years." Most states have also increased the penalties for selling or using drugs on school campuses. Laws in Illinois, New Hampshire, and Michigan call for severe penalties, inducing imprisonment, for the possession or distribution of drugs in or near schools and have lowered the current age for prosecution of juveniles as adults. Under recent "zero tolerance" initiatives, trivial forms of student misconduct that were once handled informally by teachers and school administrators are now more likely to result in police arrest and referral to juvenile or adult court. Five students in Mississippi were suspended recently and criminally charged for tossing peanuts at each other on a school bus; a peanut hit the bus driver by mistake.

Increasingly, the search efforts of police officials stationed in public schools mirror the actions of prison guards. For example, to create a drug-free environment, schools are allowing police officers to conduct random preemptive searches of students' lockers and personal property using specially trained sniff dogs. Over 1,000 schools in 14 states use drug-sniffing dogs supplied by a Texas company called Interquest Detection Canines. The profit motive is a powerful incentive to expand canine searches to schools that have no demonstrable drug problems. One school board has even formed a partnership with the U.S. Customs Department to send dogs into classrooms for drug-detection training exercises. In writing about canine searches in Boston public schools, journalist Marcia Vigue describes the following scene:

> Secrecy is the key. Students, teachers, and parents are not warned in advance; some student handbooks do not even explain that [searches] might occur from time to time. . . . During the searches, the dogs respond to German commands like "sook"—which means search—by pushing their snouts against lockers and nudging their noses into bags and coats. Sometime, after students have been told to leave, the dogs pass through classrooms and other rooms to sniff students' belongings.

The personal indignity of forcing students to submit to a suspicionless canine search is something no adult would tolerate.

Besides police controlled canine searches, schools are turning to sting operations in which undercover law enforcement officials pretend to be students to conduct actual criminal investigations of students suspected of using or dealing drugs in the school setting. In Los Angeles, for example, undercover officers made over 200 drug buys over a five-month period at local schools. Opponents of school-based sting operations say they not only create a climate of mistrust between students and police, but also put innocent students at risk of wrongful arrest due to faulty tips and overzealous police work. When asked about his role in a recent undercover drug probe at a high school near Atlanta, a young-looking police officer who attended classes and went to parties with students replied: "I knew I had to fit in, make the kids trust me and then turn around and take them to jail."

Police have adopted other aggressive search tactics on school campuses, such as herding students into hallways for unannounced weapons searches, known as "blitz operations." At Shawnee Heights and Seaman High School in Kansas City, signs warn students driving into school parking areas that they have just consented to searches of their vehicles "with or without cause" by school administrators or police officers. Scores of other schools across the country have adopted similar vehicle search policies. Groups of students have even been strip-searched by police officers to locate money missing from a classroom. There seems to be no end in sight to the aggressive search methods police are willing to use on students in the name of safety.

The Fourth Amendment and Schools

The Fourth Amendment of the United States Constitution provides the following:

> The right of the people to be secure in their persons, houses, papers, and effects against unreasonable searches and seizures, shall not be violated, and no Warrants shall issue, but upon probable cause, supported by Oath or affirmation, and particularly describing the place to be searched, and the persons or things to be seized.

In the past, courts held that school authorities acted in loco parentis when searching students and as such were not bound by Fourth Amendment restrictions that apply to state officials.

In the 1995 landmark case of *New Jersey v. T.L.O.*, the United States Supreme Court held that the Fourth Amendment did apply to searches conducted by public school officials. The Court specifically considered the search of a student's purse by an assistant vice-principal after a teacher had discovered the student, and her friend, smoking in the school washroom in violation of school policy. Upon searching T.L.O.'s purse, the assistant vice-principal discovered cigarettes and a package of cigarette rolling papers, which to him suggested involvement with marijuana. A more extensive search revealed a small amount of marijuana, a pipe, empty plastic bags, and letters implicating T.L.O. in selling drugs. Thereafter, the police were notified and the state of New Jersey filed delinquency charges against T.L.O. for possession of marijuana with intent to sell.

On appeal, the U.S. Supreme Court ruled that school children do not waive their Fourth Amendment rights by bringing purses, books, and items necessary for personal grooming and hygiene to school. However, a certain degree of "flexibility" in school searches was deemed necessary, which made the warrant and probable cause requirements "impractical." Ultimately, the Court held that school officials need only have "reasonable suspicion" for student searches. Reasonable suspicion means that school officials "must have some [articulable] facts or knowledge that provide reasonable grounds" before conducting a search. Under *T.L.O.*, a search is reasonable if, first, the search decision is supported by reasonable suspicion and, second, the scope of the search is not "excessively intrusive" in light of the age and sex of the student and the nature of the infraction.

The *T.L.O.* decision avoided the issue of whether the probable cause or reasonable suspicion standard would apply to police searches in public schools. In the absence of a clear standard to guide police searches on school campuses, appellate courts have fashioned new criteria that give police officers the same search leeway as teachers. The case examined below, *People v. Dilworth*, is a good example.

People v. Dilworth

Kenneth Dilworth, a 15-year-old high school student in Joliet, Illinois, was arrested for drug possession by a police detective assigned full-time to a high school for teenagers with behavioral disorders. Detective Francis Ruettiger served as liaison police officer on staff at the school, but was employed by the Joliet police department. Two teachers at the school asked Ruettiger to search a student, Deshawn Weeks, for drugs. The teachers informed Ruettiger that they had overheard Weeks telling other students he had sold some drugs and would bring more drugs with him to school the next day. The detective searched Weeks, but no drugs were found. Ruettiger then escorted the boy to his locker, where the youth and 15-year-old Kenneth Dilworth began talking and giggling. Ruettiger testified he felt "like [he] was being played for a fool." The officer noticed Dilworth had a flashlight and suspected it might contain contraband. He seized it, unscrewed the top, and found cocaine. After discovering cocaine, Ruettiger chased and captured Dilworth, handcuffed him, placed him in a police vehicle, and escorted him to the Joliet police station. Dilworth was subsequently tried and found guilty in adult court for unlawful possession of a controlled substance with intent to deliver on school property. He was sentenced to a four-year term of imprisonment. Dilworth's motion to reconsider the sentence was denied.

The appellate court reversed Dilworth's conviction on the grounds that his motion to suppress evidence discovered in his flashlight should have been granted. In the opinion of the appellate court, Ruettiger's seizure and search of the flashligh were based on only an unparticularized suspicion or "hunch" and did not comport with any standard of reasonableness for searches and seizures of students and their effects by state officials.

However, a divided Illinois Supreme Court in a four-to-three decision reversed the appellate court decision. Claiming that a flashlight in the context of an alternative school could reasonably be construed to be a weapon, the court affirmed Ruettiger's search as reasonable. The majority reasoned that lower expectations of privacy in the school setting, discussed in *T.L.O.*, supported a sharp departure from the probable cause standard for a school liaison officer. Even though detective Ruettiger was employed by the Joliet police department and performed duties at the school more in line with a regular law enforcement officer than a school official, the court maintained the search was proper.

The *Dilworth* decision stands in stark opposition to Fourth Amendment precedents that require the probable cause test to be met when evidence from a search by a law enforcement official forms the basis of a criminal prosecution. For example, in *A.J.M. v. State* (1993), the *T.L.O.* standard does not apply to a search by a sheriff's officer who was serving as a School Resource Officer and was asked to conduct a search by the school principal; in *F.P. v. State* (1988), the *T.L.O.* standard does not apply where a search is carried out at the behest of police.

Justice Nickels, dissenting in *Dilworth*, severely criticized the majority for lowering the search standard for a school police officer when he stated:

> I cannot agree with the majority that a police officer whose self-stated primary duty is to investigate and prevent criminal activity may search a student on school grounds on a lesser [F]ourth amendment standard than probable cause merely because the police officer is permanently assigned to the school and is listed in the student handbook as a member of the school staff. The majority's departure from a unanimous line of Federal and State decisions places form over substance and opens the door for widespread abuse and erosion of students' [F]ourth amendment rights to be free from unreasonable searches and seizures by law enforcement officers.

The *Dilworth* decision is representative of a series of recent cases in which trial and appellate courts have lowered the bar for student searches by police officers. Instead of protecting schoolchildren from arbitrary police intrusion, courts have given law enforcement officials the widest latitude to search students. For example, state appellate courts have redefined police search conduct as "minor" or "incidental" to justify application of the reasonable suspicion standard. Appellate courts have also suggested that the lesser reasonable suspicion test should be applied when police search at the request of school officials or are present when school authorities engage in a search. Courts have even upheld dragnet suspicionless searches of school lockers and police-directed canine searches of students' property with no warnings. Due to these decisions, public school children may now be searched on less than probable cause and prosecuted in adult court with the evidence from the search.

Students Need Fourth Amendment Protection

In response to widely publicized incidents of schoolyard violence, public schools have adopted rigid and intrusive security measures that diminish the rights of students. In the name of safety, students are being spied on with hidden cameras, searched without suspicion, and subjected to unannounced locker searches by police with drug-sniffing dogs. Concurrently, federal and state lawmakers have significantly increased penalties for crimes committed on school property. Trivial forms of student misconduct that used to be handled informally by teachers and school administrators are now more likely to result in arrest and referral to a juvenile or adult court. Ironically, the current "crackdown" on schoolchildren comes at a time when the level of violence and drug use in public schools has gone down.

Because [as legal scholar Mai Linh Spencer states,] the school setting demands "constant submission to authority," and is imposing harsher criminal penalties on students who misbehave, the legal rights of schoolchildren ought to be given the highest legal protection afforded by the nation's courts. Regrettably, the opposite is true. Bowing to public fears and legislative pressures, trial and appellate courts have reduced the Fourth Amendment rights of students to an abstraction. The nation's courts no longer seem interested in scrutinizing the specific facts surrounding the search of a student to determine if police had probable cause or even reasonable suspicion. Instead, courts search for a policy justification—e.g., minimizing disruptions to school order or protecting the safety of students and teachers—to uphold the search, even when police use evidence seized under lower and increasingly porous search standards to convict minors in adult criminal court. Given the current atmosphere of widespread fear and distress precipitated by the September 11, 2001, tragedy, there is little reason to expect courts will impose any restrictions on searches in schools. Ironically, children are unsafe in public schools today not because of exposure to drugs and violence, but because they have lost their constitutional protections under the Fourth Amendment.

ORGANIZATIONS TO CONTACT

The editors have compiled the following list of organizations concerned with the issues presented in this book. The descriptions are derived from materials provided by the organizations. All have publications or information available for interested readers. The list was compiled on the date of publication of the present volume; the information provided here may change. Be aware that many organizations take several weeks or longer to respond to inquiries, so allow as much time as possible.

American Academy of Child and Adolescent Psychiatry (AACAP)
3615 Wisconsin Ave. NW, Washington, DC 20016-3007
(202) 966-7300 • fax: (202) 966-2891
Web site: www.aacap.org

AACAP is the leading national professional medical association committed to treating the 7 to 12 million American youth suffering from mental, behavioral, and developmental disorders. It publishes the monthly *Journal of the American Academy of Child and Adolescent Psychiatry* and the reports "Children and TV Violence," "Understanding Violent Behavior in Children and Adolescents," "Children and Guns," and "Bullying."

American Civil Liberties Union (ACLU)
125 Broad St., 18th Fl., New York, NY 10004
(212) 549-2500 • fax: (212) 549-2646
e-mail: aclu@aclu.org • Web site: www.aclu.org

The ACLU is a national organization that defends Americans' civil rights guaranteed in the U.S. Constitution. It works to establish equality before the law, regardless of race, color, sexual orientation, or national origin. The ACLU publishes and distributes the semiannual newsletter *Civil Liberties Alert*, policy statements, pamphlets, and reports which include "From Words to Weapons: The Violence Surrounding Our Schools" and "Ask Sybil Liberty About Your Right to Fair Treatment."

Canadians Concerned About Violence in Entertainment (C-CAVE)
167 Glen Rd., Toronto, ON M4W 2W8 Canada
(416) 961-0853 • fax: (416) 929-2720
e-mail: info@c-cave.com

C-CAVE conducts research on the harmful effects violence in the media has on society and provides its findings to the Canadian government and public. The organization's committees research issues of violence against women and children, sports violence, and pornography. C-CAVE disseminates educational materials, including periodic news updates.

Center for the Prevention of School Violence (CPSV)
1801 Mail Service Center, Raleigh, NC 27699-1801
(800) 299-6054 • (919) 733-3388 ext. 332
e-mail: jaclyn.myers@ncmail.net • Web site: www.ncdjjdp.org/cpsv

The CPSV is a primary point of contact for information, programs, and research about school violence and its prevention. As a clearinghouse, it provides information about all aspects of the problems which fall under the heading of school violence as well as information about strategies that are directed at solving these problems. Publications include statistical reports, research bul-

letins such as "Students Against Violence Everywhere: A National Profile," and
Q & A of the Month discussions such as "What are some tips on how to address
bullying?"

Mediascope
100 Universal City Plaza, Bldg. 6159, Universal City, CA 91608
(818) 733-3180 • fax: (818) 733-3181
e-mail: facts@mediascope.org • Web site: www.mediascope.org

Mediascope is a national nonprofit research and public policy organization
working to raise awareness about the way the media affects society. Founded in
1992, it encourages responsible depictions of social and health issues in film,
television, the Internet, video games, advertising, and music. Among its many
publications are *National Television Violence Study, Youth and Violent Music,
American Public Opinion on Media Violence, Crime and Violence in American
Schools,* and *Youth Violence in America.*

Morality in Media (MIM)
475 Riverside Dr., Suite 239, New York, NY 10115
(212) 870-3222 • fax: (212) 870-2765
e-mail: mim@moralityinmedia.org • Web site: www.moralityinmedia.org

Established in 1962, MIM is a national not-for-profit interfaith organization
that works to combat obscenity and violence and to uphold decency standards
in the media. It maintains the National Obscenity Law Center, a clearinghouse
of legal materials, and conducts public information programs to involve concerned citizens. Its publications include the bimonthly *Morality in Media* newsletter and the reports "Media Responsibility in a Democratic Society" and
"How Media Violence Affects Our Kids."

National Alliance for Safe Schools (NASS)
PO Box 290, Slanesville, WV 25445
(888) 510-6500 • (304) 496-8100 • fax: (304) 496-8105
e-mail: nass@raven-villages.net • Web site: www.safeschools.org

Founded in 1977 by a group of school security directors, the National Alliance
for Safe Schools was established to provide training, security assessments, and
technical assistance to school districts interested in reducing school-based
crime and violence. It publishes the book *Making Schools Safe for Students.*

National Association of School Resource Officers (NASRO)
1601 N.E. 100th St., Anthony, FL 32617
(888) 316-2776
e-mail: resourcer@aol.com • Web site: www.nasro.org

The National Association of School Resource Officers is the first nonprofit
training organization made up of liaison officers currently assigned to a school
community. Its mission is to break down barriers between law enforcement
and youth by establishing better communication about the legal system. Its
official publication is *Resourcer.*

National Congress of Black Women (NCBW)
8484 Georgia Ave., Suite 40, Silver Spring, MD 20910
(877) 274-1198 • (301) 562-8000 • fax: (301) 562-8303
e-mail: info@npcbw.org • Web site: www.npcbw.org

The NCBW supports the advancement of African American women in politics
and government. The congress also engages in research on critical issues that
affect the quality of life of African American women and youth. Through its

Commission on Entertainment, the NCBW campaigns against the glorification of violence, misogyny, pornography, and drugs in popular entertainment. It runs a "Save Our Schools" commission and publishes project reports on its Web site, including "Crusading Against Gangsta/Porno Rap."

National Criminal Justice Reference Service (NCJRS)
PO Box 6000, Rockville, MD 20849-6000
(800) 851-3420 • (301) 519-5500 • fax: (301) 519-5212
e-mail: askncjrs@ncjrs.org • Web site: www.ncjrs.org

A component of the Office of Justice Programs of the U.S. Department of Justice, the NCJRS supports research on crime, criminal behavior, and crime prevention. The service acts as a clearinghouse for criminal justice information for researchers and other interested individuals. Among the numerous reports it publishes and distributes are "Bullying Prevention Is Crime Prevention," "Are Our Children Safe at School?" and "Deadly Lessons: Understanding Lethal School Violence."

National School Safety Center (NSSC)
141 Duesenberg Dr., Suite 11, Westlake Village, CA 91362
(805) 373-9977 • fax: (805) 373-9277
e-mail: info@nssc1.org • Web site: www.nssc1.org

The NSSC is a research organization that studies school crime and violence, including hate crimes. The center's mandate is to focus national attention on cooperative solutions to problems which disrupt the educational process. NSSC provides training, technical assistance, legal and legislative aid, and publications and films toward this cause. Its publications include numerous resource papers, the books *Set Straight on Bullies* and *Gangs in Schools: Breaking Up Is Hard to Do*, and the news journal *School Safety*, published three times a year, along with six *School Safety Updates*.

Office of Juvenile Justice and Delinquency Prevention (OJJDP)
810 Seventh St. NW, Washington, DC 20531
(202) 307-5911 • fax: (202) 307-2093
e-mail: askjj@ncjrs.org • Web site: http://ojjdp.ncjrs.org

As the primary federal agency charged with monitoring and improving the juvenile justice system, the OJJDP develops and funds programs on juvenile justice. Among its goals are the prevention and control of illegal drug use and serious crime by juveniles. Through its Juvenile Justice Clearinghouse, the OJJDP distributes fact sheets and reports such as "Combating Fear and Restoring Safety in Schools," "Fighting Juvenile Gun Violence," "Violence After School," and the "Annual Report on School Safety."

BIBLIOGRAPHY

Books

Bob Algozzine and Pam Kay, eds.	*Preventing Problem Behaviors: A Handbook of Successful Prevention Strategies.* Thousand Oaks, CA: Corwin Press and Council for Exceptional Children, 2002.
Allan L. Beane	*The Bully-Free Classroom: Over 100 Tips and Strategies for Teachers K–8.* Minneapolis: Free Spirit, 1999.
Fred Bemak and Susan Keys	*Violent and Aggressive Youth: Intervention and Prevention Strategies for Changing Times.* Thousand Oaks, CA: Corwin, 2000.
Joan N. Burstyn et al., eds.	*Preventing Violence in Schools: A Challenge to American Democracy.* Mahwah, NJ: Lawrence Erlbaum Associates, 2001.
Thomas Capozolli et al.	*Kids Killing Kids: Managing Violence and Gangs in School.* Boca Raton, FL: Saint Lucie, 1999.
Ronnie Casella	*"Being Down": Challenging Violence in Urban Schools.* New York: Teachers College Press, 2001.
Delbert S. Elliott, Beatrix A. Hamburg, and Kirk R. Williams, eds.	*Violence in American Schools: A New Perspective.* London: Cambridge University Press, 1998.
Albert H. Fein	*There and Back Again: School Shootings as Experienced by School Leaders.* Lanham, MD: Scarecrow, 2003.
Mary Susan Fishbaugh, Terry R. Berkeley, and Gwen Schroth	*Ensuring Safe School Environments: Exploring Issues— Seeking Solutions.* Mahwah, NJ: Lawrence Erlbaum Associates, 2003.
Irwin A. Hyman and Pamela A. Snook	*Dangerous Schools: What We Can Do About the Physical and Emotional Abuse of Our Children.* San Francisco: Jossey-Bass, 1999.
Tony L. Jones	*Effective Response to School Violence: A Guide for Educators and Law Enforcement Personnel.* Springfield, IL: Charles C. Thomas, 2001.
Tricia S. Jones and Randy Compton, eds.	*Kids Working It Out: Stories and Strategies for Making Peace in Our Schools.* San Francisco: Jossey-Bass, 2002.
Jaana Juvonen and Sandra Graham, eds.	*Peer Harassment in School: The Plight of the Vulnerable and Victimized.* New York: Guilford, 2001.
H. Roy Kaplan	*Failing Grades: How Schools Breed Frustration, Anger, and Violence, and How to Prevent It.* Lanham, MD: Rowman & Littlefield, 2004.
Mark H. Moore et al., eds.	*Deadly Lesson: Understanding Lethal School Violence.* Washington, DC: National Academies Press, 2002.
Allen J. Ottens and Kathy Hotelling, eds.	*Sexual Violence on Campus: Policies, Programs, and Perspectives.* New York: Springer, 2001.

Daya Singh Sandhu   *Violence in American Schools: A Practical Guide for*
and Cheryl Blalock   *Counselors.* Alexandria, VA: American Counseling
Aspy, eds.   Association, 2000.

Denise Smith, ed.   *Bulletproof Vests vs. the Ethic of Care: Which Strategy Is*
                       Your School Using? Lanham, MD: Scarecrow, 2003.

Nan Stein   *Classrooms and Courtrooms: Facing Sexual Harassment in*
                       K–12 Schools. New York: Teachers College Press, 1999.

U.S. Department   *Early Warning Timely Response: A Guide to Safe Schools,*
of Education   U.S. Department of Education, 1998.

Julie A. Weber   *Failure to Hold: The Politics of School Violence.* Lanham,
                       MD: Rowman & Littlefield, 2003.

Roberta Wetzel and   *Student-Generated Sexual Harassment in Secondary*
Nina W. Brown   *Schools.* Westport, CT: Bergin & Garvey, 2000.

Jerry Wilde   *Anger Management in Schools: Alternatives to Student*
                       Violence. Lanham, MD: Scarecrow, 2002.

Periodicals

Julie Adams   "Seasonal Trends in School Violence," *Psychology*
                       Today, March/April 2002.

John M. Beam   "The Blackboard Jungle: Tamer than You Think," *New*
                       York Times, January 20, 2004.

Judith A. Browne,   "Zero Tolerance: Unfair, with Little Recourse," *New*
Daniel J. Losen, and   *Directions for Youth Development*, Winter 2001.
Johanna Wald

Katherine T. Bucher   "Challenges and Suggestions for Safe Schools,"
and Lee M. Manning   *Clearing House*, January/February 2003.

A.W. Dodd   "Making Schools Safe for All Students: Why Schools
                       Need to Teach More than the 3 R's," *NASSP Bulletin*,
                       March 2000.

Annette Fuentes   "Discipline and Punish," *Nation*, December 15, 2003.

M.J. Furlong,   "Predicting School Weapon Possession: A Secondary
M.P. Bates, and   Analysis of the Youth Risk Behavior Surveillance
D.C. Smith   Survey," *Psychology in the Schools*, March 2001.

Elissa Gootman   "Police to Guard 12 City Schools Cited as Violent,"
                       New York Times, January 6, 2004.

I.M. Harris   "Peace-Building Responses to School Violence," *NASSP*
                       Bulletin, March 2000.

David M. Herszenhorn   "Assaults on Teachers Are Increasing, Union Says,"
                       New York Times, May 20, 2003.

J.D. Heyman and   "Did Bullying—or a Mother's Neglect—Drive a
Marianne V. Stochmal   12-Year-Old Boy to Suicide?" *People Weekly*, October
                       20, 2003.

F.Q. Hoang   "Addressing School Violence," *FBI Law Enforcement*
                       Bulletin, August 2001.

P.J. Huffstutter   "A High School Where the Censorship Is Pervasive,"
                            Los Angeles Times, September 8, 2002.

I.A. Hyman and   "Dangerous Schools and What You Can Do About
P.A. Snook   Them," *Phi Delta Kappan*, March 2000.

Michael D. Lemonick   "Germany's Columbine," *Time*, May 6, 2002.
and Charles P. Wallace

Susannah Meadows   "Ghosts of Columbine," *Newsweek*, November 3,
                            2003.

Susannah Meadows   "Why Matthew Snapped," *Newsweek*, July 21, 2003.

Emily Mitchell   "How to Keep the Peace," *Time*, September 13, 1999.

Jodie Morse   "The Perception Gap: School Violence," *Time*, April
                            24, 2000.

Laura Pulfer   "Sean Graves's New World," *Rosie*, May 2002.

Mindy Sink   "It Still Hurts: For Columbine Students, the Struggle
                            Isn't Over," *Upfront Online*, April 16, 2001.

Russell J. Skiba and   "Zero Tolerance, Zero Evidence: An Analysis of School
Kimberly Knesting   Disciplinary Practice," *New Directions for Youth
                            Development*, Winter 2001.

Robert Tomsho   "Schools' Efforts to Protect Gays Face Opposition,"
                            Wall Street Journal, February 20, 2003.

Tom Weir   "Move Afoot to Educate Teachers on Hazing," *USA
                            Today*, December 19, 2003.

Emily Yellin   "Terror in Littleton: The Familiar Sorrow; as Jonesboro
                            Shooting Fades, a Killer's Family Still Lives It," *New
                            York Times*, April 27, 1999.

INDEX

abuse, prevention of, 143–47
academic achievement, 17–18, 45, 63
acceptance, 129–37, 143–47
accommodation, 112
active listening, 120, 124–26
administrators, school
    intervention by, 24, 29–30, 45,
        51–53
    responsibilities of, 119–37, 143–47
    as targets, 15–16
adolescents, 39, 67–77, 97–100,
    102–106, 111–12, 138–42
adults, relationships with, 144
    see also families; parents; teachers
African Americans. See blacks
aggression, 62–66, 108, 110, 115–16,
    130, 138–42
    see also behavior, antisocial;
        bullying
A.J.M. v. State, 159
Alaska, shootings in, 80–81
alcohol abuse, 18–19, 39–40, 70
American Academy of Child and
    Adolescent Psychiatry, 47–50
American Psychological Association,
    47
anger, 29, 83–84
    management of, 110, 112–13,
        120–21, 124
antisocial personality disorder, 47–48
arrests, 19, 39–40, 42, 62–63, 65
attacks, planning of, 15–16, 20–24
attention deficit hyperactivity
    disorder (ADHD), 62, 64–65
attention-getting, as motive, 21

Baldwin, James, 134
Bang Bang You're Dead (play), 98–100
Beast, The (film), 98
Beger, Randall R., 152
behavior
    antisocial, 37, 40–42, 45–53, 60–62,
        65, 138–42
    as warning sign, 13, 17–18,
        20–23, 27
    criminal, 19, 27, 46–47, 54–56, 64
    risk-taking, 65
bisexuals, 88–96, 129–37
blacks, 9–11, 76, 153
    as perpetrators, 16, 37, 71

blitz operations, 156–57
bombs, 23, 61
books, 19
Booth, Stephanie, 86
boredom, 76
Bower, Amanda, 79
boys, 37, 115–16, 132–33, 144
    as perpetrators, 15–16, 39–42, 55,
        65, 67–77
brain, development of, 64
Brazill, Nathaniel, 79–80, 82–83
bullying, 9, 25–34, 62, 80, 84,
    144–47
    homophobic, 67–77, 88–96
    see also behavior, antisocial;
        harassment
Burning Season, The (film), 98
Burstyn, Joan N., 119

canine searches, 156, 159–60
Carneal, Michael, 69, 74, 82–84
Caucasians. See whites
causes, 9–10, 68–72, 76, 83–84
Centers for Disease Control and
    Prevention (CDC), 54
child abuse, 27, 64, 69–70, 141
children, 38–39, 58–66, 97–100,
    138–47
classrooms, 121–23
Clayton, Bill, 88–96
Clayton, Gabi, 88
collaboration, 126–27
Columbine High School (Colorado),
    9–11, 14, 37, 75–76, 81, 83–84, 106
community, 9–10, 146–47
concentration, problems with, 65
conduct disorder (CD), 47–48, 51, 64
conflict resolution, 108–28, 138–42
Conyers, Georgia, shootings in, 63,
    82, 99
cooperative learning, 124–25, 146–47
coping, difficulty with, 19–20, 49,
    111–12, 132
Cordova, Victor, 83, 85
counseling, 56, 133–36, 141, 143–47
court decisions, 152–53, 157–60
crimes, 36–38, 42, 155
criminals, 10–11
Crutcher, Chris, 102
curriculum, 124–25

Daunic, Ann P., 108
Davis, Jacob, 82–83
deaths, 35–38, 69
demographics, 16–17, 39, 55, 59
depression, 18–20, 22, 45, 49–51, 79,
    83–84
    bullying as cause of, 27, 31, 33, 89,
    92–93
desperation, as motive, 21–22
detention, 108
DiGiulio, Robert C., 35
Dilworth, Kenneth, 158
disabilities, 58–66, 123
discipline, 17–18, 29, 104–105,
    121–23, 148–51, 155–56, 160
    see also detention; expulsion;
    suspension
diversity training, 129–37, 145
domestic violence, 27, 141
dropouts, 27, 39, 62–63
drug abuse, 18–19, 39–40, 69–70

education/educators, 40, 123–24,
    132–33, 138–42
    see also administrators, school;
    teachers
Education for All Handicapped
    Children Act, 59
elementary schools, 30, 144–45, 149
Elliott, Gail Pursell, 31
Eminem, 73
emotional disturbance (ED), 47,
    62–63
ethnicity, 9–11, 41, 71, 76, 123, 129,
    133
expulsion, 18, 37, 40, 60, 153
extracurricular activities, 17, 146–47
Extremities (film), 98

families, 17, 69–70, 79, 81–82,
    139–41
    as sources for guns, 54–55
    violence in, 45, 76
Feris, Nathan, 27
Fields, Lynette, 148
fights, 148–51
films. See movies
Final Report and Findings of the Safe
    School Initiative, 13–24, 58–59, 66
firearms. See guns
flashbacks, 79–80, 85
Florida, school security in, 40
foster homes, 17
Fourth Amendment (U.S.
    Constitution), 152–53, 157–60

F.P. v. State, 159
friends, 28, 79, 81–82, 143–47
    intervention by, 86–87
    as sources for guns, 54–56
fringe groups, 17
frontal lobe dysfunction, 64

gangs, 55–56, 149
Garrett, Anne G., 138
Gay, Lesbian, Straight Educators
    Network (GLSEN), 132, 134, 136
"gay-baiting," 68, 72–76, 88–96, 132,
    135–36
gender, 26, 40–41, 67–77, 123, 144
girls, 40–41, 115–16
    as perpetrators, 42, 55, 70
Golden, Andrew, 82, 85
gossiping, 115
government, responsibilities of, 100
grades, 17–18, 135
    see also academic achievement
Grant, Carl A., 123–24
grief, 48–49, 51
grievances, 21
Gun-Free Schools Act, 60
guns, 15, 22–23, 25, 60–61
    availability of, 13, 39, 54–57, 69,
    76
    ownership of, 9, 100

handguns, 15, 57, 71, 119
    see also guns
Hanser, Sam, 135
harassment, 18, 23, 25–30, 115–16
    homophobic, 68, 76, 88–96, 129,
    135–36
    prevention of, 143–47
Harris, Eric, 9, 70, 75, 80–81
Harvey Milk School (New York City),
    131
hate crimes, 88–96, 135
Head, Brian, 27
heterosexuals, 73, 76, 130, 132
high schools, 9–11, 36–37, 67, 71, 76,
    144, 149
    bullying in, 25, 27
    see also middle schools; names of
    specific high schools
Hispanics, 16
homicides, 22, 35–41, 54–56, 69, 141,
    154
    see also suicide
homophobia, 67–77, 88–96, 129–37
homosexuality, 129–37
hyperactivity, 65

imprisonment, 37–38, 40, 43, 79–85
impulsivity, 64–65
inclusiveness, 119, 133–35
individualized education program
 (IEP), 59–61
Individuals with Disabilities Act
 (IDEA), 59–62
Internet, 69–71, 134–35
intervention, 23–24, 42, 120, 148–51
 for at-risk children, 61, 138–42
 see also prevention
isolation, 17, 79, 102–106, 130–31,
 143–47
 as result of bullying, 31, 33

Japan, bullying in, 25
jock culture, 75–77
Johnson, Mitchell, 82, 85
Jonesboro, Arkansas, shootings in,
 13, 63, 70, 82, 98, 133
juvenile delinquency, 38–39, 62–65,
 69, 141
Juvenile Justice Bill, 61

Kansas City, Kansas, school security
 in, 156–57
Kimmel, Michael S., 67
Kinkel, Kip, 81, 83
Klebold, Dylan, 9, 75, 80–81
knives, 23, 41

lateral thinking, 122
law enforcement officials, 23–24, 40,
 152–60
learning disabilities (LD), 62–64
legislation, 59–61
lesbians, 129–37
Like Totally Weird (play), 97
Littleton, Colorado, shootings in,
 9–11, 13, 63, 70, 99–100
loners, 17
Lorenz, Konrad, 32–33
Louisiana, school security in, 155
Loukaitis, Barry, 74, 102–103
Luvox, 65

Mahler, Matthew, 67
males. See boys
masculinity, 67–77, 144
Massachusetts, gay rights in, 135–37
Mastrosimone, William, 97
McCormick Middle School (South
 Carolina), 30
media, 10–11, 19, 32, 35–43, 69–71
 violence in, 97–100, 110

mental illness, 18–19, 27, 31, 76,
 83–84
Michigan, school security in, 38, 155
middle schools, 25–27, 30, 111–16
minorities, 10–11, 133, 136
Mississippi, school security in,
 155–56
mobbing, 31–34
 see also bullying
movies, 19, 69, 71, 76, 97–100
multicultural education, 123–24
murders. See homicides
music, 71, 98
Myers-Briggs Type Indicator (MBTI),
 133–34
myths, 35–42

National Longitudinal Transition
 Study, 62
Native Americans, 16–17, 134
Natural Born Killers (film), 97
neglect, 17, 64, 70, 141, 146
negotiation, 29, 110, 120–21, 124
neurological impairment, 64–65
New Jersey v. T.L.O., 157–58

Oakley, Ben, 75
Office of Community Oriented
 Policing Services (COPS), 155
oppositional defiant disorder (ODD),
 47–48, 51, 64
Osterman, Karen F., 143

Paducah, Kentucky, shootings in, 13,
 63, 69–70, 74, 82, 98–100
parents, 22, 45, 70, 79, 81–82
 responsibilities of, 28–29, 43, 100,
 119–33
 as sources for guns, 54–56
Parents and Friends of Lesbians and
 Gays (PFLAG), 132
Pearl, Mississippi, shootings in, 63,
 70, 74, 82
peer mediation, 108–18, 120–21
 see also conflict resolution
Pennington, Gary Scott, 74
People v. Dilworth, 158–59
perpetrators, 10–11, 15–34, 58,
 70–71, 79–85
 age of, 38–39, 54–55
 characteristics of, 13–24, 26–27
 emotional disabilities of, 62–63, 65
personality disorders, 47–51, 83–84
"Picnic, The" (short story), 134
Pope, Mark, 129

posttraumatic stress disorder (PTSD), 48–49, 51, 89
preschool programs, 140
prevention, 40–41, 45, 52–57, 66, 86, 109–12
    of bullying, 30, 32, 34
    whole school approach to, 119–28, 140–41
    see also conflict resolution; intervention; zero-tolerance policies
prisons, 38, 40, 43, 79–85
Project Pursuit, 140
Project 10 (California), 131
Prozac, 65
psychoaffective education, 132–33
psychotropic drugs, 19, 65, 84
Pulp Fiction (film), 97
punishment, 79–85, 152
    see also discipline

Ramsey, Evan, 74, 80–81
recognition, as motive, 21
rehabilitation, 84–85
rejection, 9, 143–47
relationships, 17–18, 20, 144
relatives, 13, 54–56
remorse, 79–85
resiliency, 52
restlessness, 65
revenge, as motive, 21, 26, 31, 33
rifles, 15, 71
    see also guns
risk factors, 45–53, 138–40
    see also warning signs
Ritalin, 65
Roche, Timothy, 79
Ruettiger, Francis, 158–59

safety. See schools, safety of; security measures
Santee, California, shootings in, 73–74, 81, 83, 86–87
Saving Private Ryan (film), 100
schizophrenia, 83–84
School Resource Officers (SROs), 154–55, 159
schools
    safety of, 35–36, 39, 60, 67–68, 120–21, 148, 152–54
    violence in, 13–24, 58–59, 66, 71–72
search-and-seizure protections, 152–60
security measures, 41–42, 152–55, 159–60

self-esteem, 26, 28, 51, 104, 111, 130, 133
self-mutilation, 48, 50–51
sexual abuse, 89
sexual orientation, 129–37, 145
Shoels, Isaiah, 9
shooters. See perpetrators
shootings. See attacks, planning of; homicides
shotguns, 15
    see also guns
Skarbek, Denise (Smith), 58
Sleeter, Christine E., 123–24
Smart Start, 140
Smith, Stephen W., 108
Smith-Heavenrich, Sue, 25
Soaring High, 140
social reconstructionist education, 123–24
Solomon, T.J., 82, 84–85
special education, 59–60
Springfield, Oregon, shootings in, 13, 63, 70
statistics, 14–16, 59, 72
    of bullying, 25–26
    of crimes, 35–39, 54–56, 62, 69
    of security measures, 153–54
"stay-put" rule, 59–61
stealing, 62, 154
Stevens, Josh, 86
Stevens, Rebecca, 119
sting operations, 156
students
    intervention by, 22, 24, 86–87, 113–28
    rights of, 152–60
    as targets, 15–16
suicide, 21–22, 24–25, 35, 38, 41, 54–56
    attempts at, 18–19, 27, 79–80, 135
    bullying as cause of, 33, 88–96
    risk factors for, 48, 50–51
suspension, 18, 37–38, 40, 43, 108, 153
    of children with special needs, 59–61
Sweden, bullying in, 33–34
Synectics, 122

tardiness, 37–38
Taylor, Curtis, 27
teachers, 22, 104–105
    intervention by, 24, 29–30, 45, 51–53, 148–51
    responsibilities of, 119–37, 143–47

as targets, 15–16, 20
Teaching Respect for All (workshop), 132, 134
teasing, 18, 72, 104, 106
see also bullying
teenagers. *See* adolescents
television, 71, 76
Tewksbury Memorial High School (Massachusetts), 153
thefts, 62, 154
threats, 22, 50, 115
Title I Pre-Kindergarten, 140
Todd, Evan, 75
tolerance, 30, 119, 123, 131, 135, 143–47
toys, 26
transgender youth, 129–37
Trickey, Seth, 84–85
truancy, 37–38, 135

United Kingdom, bullying in, 33
U.S. Department of Education, 13, 58–59, 66
U.S. Secret Service, 13, 58–59, 66

vehicle searches, 157

victimization, 144–47, 154
victims, 10, 16, 25–34, 40–41, 71
ages of, 39, 54–55
video games, 19, 69, 71, 76, 98–99

warning signs, 20–23, 45–53, 81, 86–87
weapons, 15–16, 23, 41–42, 54–55
Weeks, Deshawn, 158–59
whites, 37, 76, 153
as perpetrators, 9–11, 16, 55, 67, 71
whole school approach, 119–28
Williams, Charles "Andy," 73–74, 81, 86–87
Williams, Kimberly M., 45
Willow Creek Elementary School (Colorado), 30
Woodham, Luke, 74, 82–84
writings, personal, 19, 22
Wurst, Andrew, 85

youth. *See* adolescents; children

zero-tolerance policies, 40–42, 106, 153, 155–56
see also discipline